Under His Wings ~ Lessons From God Learned While Watching the Birds

Joy DeKok

Under His Wings is dedicated to my parents, Ruth and Clarence Pater, who encouraged my love for the birds. And, to my husband, Jon, who keeps me supplied with bird food, a wonderful fountain for our feathered friends, and for listening to me talk about my encounters with them.

With special thanks to Cristine Bolley. Several years ago, I hurried to my last class at the Florida Christian Writer's Conference tired, and uncertain of my future as a published author. Cristine was teaching and although I don't remember the title of the workshop, in a few words she would change my life. She mentioned, casually, that if anyone had any bird stories, she had an idea for a compilation devotional. I wrote down her contact information in my notes stunned. I had dozens of stories in my journal at home. Could this be *it*?

I sent Cris ten stories. She emailed and asked if I had a few more. I sent them to her. Soon, she let me know she'd found a publisher for them and that the book would be titled *Under His Wings*.

Together we worked hard to transform my journal entries into devotionals.

I'm grateful.

Author Update

Ten years have passed since *Under His Wings* first went into print. Publishing has changed since then. When the publisher took it out of print, I considered putting the stories away. However, readers kept asking for it, and most let me know they'd enjoy it as an e-book. I couldn't refuse their generous requests.

Although the stories, lessons, and scriptures are timeless, I chose to revise the book slightly.

Many readers have written and asked for a second devotional. I'm delighted to share that God has continued to teach me about Himself through the birds, bugs, and animals of His creation. *Winged & Wild* is being written, and I hope to release it in a year or so. God has been tender and generous in His lessons to me. He has used raccoons, tree frogs, chipmunks, June bugs, a spider, deer, dragonflies, and wild turkeys—to name a few—to take me into a closer walk with Him. Oh—and a fossilized sea snail.

I have a special request: If you enjoy Under His Wings, ***please praise Him***. Whatever talent you discover in these stories, came from Him. So did the birds He has sent to teach and bless me. I'm one vessel He is using to tell His love story. There is one key message in every one of the essays in this book: He loves you and me. James 4:8a says, "Draw near to God, and He will draw near to you." One way He and I do this is through the wonderful combination of His Word and His birds. It's my prayer you will enjoy His presence in each story.

May you be blessed, and may God be glorified,

Joy DeKok

March 2013

"Are not five sparrows

sold for two pennies?

And [yet] not one of them

is forgotten or uncared for

in the presence of God."

LUKE 12:6 AMPLIFIED

"Hope is the thing with feathers
That perches in the soul.
And sings the tune
Without the words,
and never stops at all."

Emily Dickinson

TABLE OF CONTENTS

A Note from Joy

My mom and I often watch the hummingbirds at my feeders as we visit with each other. One day, a tiny bird suddenly took a wrong turn and flew into the window. We rushed outside to see if anything could be done for it.

The female ruby-throated hummingbird lay motionless on the deck floor. Her neck was bent at a strange angle.

"Gently rub her back," Mom told me. I sat down beside the bird, fearing my touch could cause more injury. With one finger, I rubbed the bird's tiny back and prayed out loud, "Lord, please heal this creature. You made her and know that we need You right now!"

A few seconds later, the bird moved its head into a different position. Then she fluttered her wings. She was alive! The new position allowed me to rub her chest. The bird settled in toward my touch and went to sleep. I picked her up and placed her in the palm of my hand. She rested there, blinked a couple of times, and then flew to a nearby branch. Soon she flew to the feeder for a drink.

Looking back at this moment, I remember the awe I felt for the Lord, Who had answered my prayer for a hummingbird. As I held her in the palm of my hand, I was deeply aware that He holds me in His. Sometimes life is full of more falls than flying. When down, we can call out to the Lord for help.

Just as God knew the tiny bird—even to the number of her iridescent feathers—He knows us, too—even the number of hairs on our heads. He knows our anxieties and sorrows, and the joys and victories He has planned for us. He is an ever-present help in trouble, who promises to answer us when we call upon Him.

Under His Wings is a collection of my personal experiences with birds, and the precious lessons God taught me about Himself through them. Each story is formatted in an easy to read and apply devotional style.

The *Bird Feeder* section offers a Bible verse to meditate upon while considering the truth of the story.

The *Birdbath* section is a verse to refresh your soul.

The *Birdhouse section,* is a scripture for you to ponder or pray.

For the Birds is where you'll find bits of information on feeding birds, watching them, and resources you might enjoy.

A Drink of Dew

I fill our birdbaths in the morning. The moist grass soaks my shoes while my feathered friends whistle and sing from nearby branches. When I finish, they flit about, taking turns drinking the fresh water.

When it's a busy time at the birdbath, the goldfinches and chickadees prefer to get their morning drinks a different way. The finches work the blades of grass for precious drops of dew. They stretch their necks as their tiny beaks move up the slender strands of green. On the nearby trees, black-capped chickadees maneuver for the best spot to reach the glistening beads of moisture on the leaves—even if it means hanging upside down to do it.

Each morning, my soul thirsts for time with God. With a hot cup of coffee within reach, I can drink deeply from the Bible. The verses of His living Word work their way into my soul and teach me about Him.

Sometimes the words pierce my heart and ready my soul to admit my mistakes. Most often the words remind me of God's unfailing love and provision. After drinking in His good news and soaking in the truth of His love, I begin my day refreshed—not because of anything I've done, but because of the power in His Word.

Now and then, I'm not able to spend a lot of time reading my Bible, but like the finches and

3

chickadees, I can still find refreshment. This usually means reaching into my Bible for a verse or two I've underlined. I carry the encouragement, strength, and peace I find there into my day.

Bird Feeder:

"Jesus stood and said in a loud voice, 'If anyone is thirsty, let him come to me and drink. Whoever believes in me, as the Scripture has said, streams of living water will flow from within him.'" (John 7:37–38)

Birdbath:

"That person is like a tree planted by streams of water, which yields its fruit in season and whose leaf does not wither— whatever they do prospers." (Psalm 1:3)

Birdhouse:

"I spread out my hands to you; I thirst for you like a parched land." (Psalm 143:6)

For the Birds:

A shallow pie pan filled with fresh water on the ground will be enjoyed by finches, chickadees, redpolls, and sparrows of all kinds. Running water from a sprinkler or fountain provides a cool drink and a bath for robins, bluebirds, finches, orioles, and others.

A Lesson in Love

Upset with my husband, I stormed outside to cool off. I sat in my favorite chair on our deck, with my arms crossed and my jaws clenched. I watched as a pair of cardinals landed at the feeders. The female approached first. When she was sure it was safe, she called to her mate. In a brilliant flash, he joined her and immediately reached for a sunflower seed. "Just like a man!" I fumed.

To my surprise, he broke open the seed and fed it to his mate. She returned the favor. Between bites, they gently rubbed beaks then flew off together. All the books I'd read on marriage were not as profound as the lesson the redbirds taught me that day. In their normal routine of eating, the cardinals illustrated devotion and honor. My anger dissipated as quickly as it had risen.

Shame and longing to be forgiven for my hasty anger sent me racing back into the house. While calling my husband's name, I cried out to God in my heart, begging His forgiveness, too.

Later, that summer, a pair of cardinals brought their young to the same feeder. The female stood guard over her family while the male patiently taught the demanding little birds the art of seed cracking. From time to time, the female came in for a seed then headed back to her perch. Neither bird hesitated to serve their young or each other. For them, it meant survival; for me, it was a lesson in love.

Bird Feeder:

"You, my brothers, were called to be free. But do not use your freedom to indulge the sinful nature; rather, serve one another in love." (Galatians 5:13)

Birdbath:

"Love must be sincere. Hate what is evil; cling to what is good. Be devoted to one another in love. Honor one another above yourselves." (Romans 12:9-10)

Birdhouse:

"Be kind and compassionate to one another, forgiving each other, just as in Christ God forgave you." (Ephesians 4:32)

For the Birds:

At least forty species of birds will eat black-oil sunflower seeds that can be purchased inexpensively in large quantities. Striped sunflower seed has a tougher shell and is more suitable for larger birds. Cracked corn is a favorite addition. The new "patio or garden" mixes leave less mess and often include dried fruits so many birds enjoy.

Apple Blossom Time

The sweet scent of apple blossoms filled the air after a gentle rain. A quiet, warm, breeze carried the fragrance into the house through my opened windows.

All at once, the air was filled with the familiar sound of many birds. I raced out of the house just as my husband stepped out of his shop. The birds' songs were so loud he had heard them above the clamor of his work. He looked at me with eyebrows raised.

"Cedar waxwings," I whispered.

We headed to the other side of the garage, where the sound came from. The apple tree was full of hungry cedar waxwings. The tired and gentle birds let us get close to them while they devoured the blossoms. We let them feast as we enjoyed their closeness.

As I turned away, a dart of deep blue near the feeders caught my attention. A little indigo bunting settled in to eat thistle seed. I sat on my chair near him and marveled that he had overcome his shyness to visit our feeder. This delightful songster is often seen along roadsides where they feed on bugs and seeds. Today his chosen lunch was thistle seed at our house.

Suddenly, a flash of red, brighter than a cardinal, drew my attention to our crab apple tree. There I saw a scarlet tanager resting among the pink blossoms.

I knew the indigo buntings and scarlet tanagers were regulars in our woods, but I'd never seen either one. I also loved the cedar waxwings and longed to see them again. So, I prayed and asked God to send these birds into my life. He brought them all in one day. His answer to my prayer felt intensely personal and loving.

When the birds moved on for the day, our yard was strangely quiet, and we missed their songs and color. However, the gentle joy of that moment lingers in our hearts even now, many years later. I remember thinking that God's answer to my prayer was so very kind, and that He had been good to me. My heart overflowed with peace, thanksgiving, and praise.

Bird Feeder:

"Give thanks to the LORD, for he is good; his love endures forever." (Psalm 106:1)

Bird Bath:

"I will praise you, LORD, with all my heart; I will tell of all the marvelous things you have done. I will be filled with joy because of you. I will sing praises to your name, O Most High." (Psalm 9:1-2 NLT)

Birdhouse:

"The LORD is righteous in everything he does; he is filled with kindness. The LORD is close to all who call on him, yes, to all who call on him in truth." (Psalm 145:17-18)

For the Birds:

Cedar Waxwings fly north to breed and can often be
seen in woods and orchards. These delightful birds
are fond of nesting in evergreens. They are drawn to
berry producing shrubs and can be seen swallowing
the berries whole. Sometimes they pick the fruit by
"hovering" near it. They will also sit in the trees and
bushes to dine. For protein, they feast on bugs, and
have been seen skimming over water to catch them.
They are social birds who live in flocks like starlings
and blackbirds.

Attempted Break-In

"Did you see the police cars in the driveway?" our neighbor Don asked when I answered his knock on our door.

"No," I responded with peaked interest.

Only four houses lined the gravel road we lived by, and police cars were not the norm. My neighbor went on to explain the damage done to his back door. Large chunks of wood littered the deck, and it looked like someone had used a chisel to get in the house.

"Apparently the intruder fled when he heard me inside," he concluded. Someone had told him that criminals often return to the scene of the crime when they don't get what they were after. Don was determined to protect his house from any further invasion. Unsettled, we returned to our homes, and I made sure the lock was secure behind me.

The intruder did indeed return and tried diligently to finish what he had started. It was only a few days later when my neighbor heard a loud pounding again at the patio door. Surprised by the boldness of the thief returning in daylight, yet determined to stop the robber once and for all, Don crept quietly to the door. Suddenly eye-to-eye with his destructive intruder, my neighbor sighed with relief and grinned at the pileated woodpecker perched on the deck door handle.

The bird was shredding what was left of the cedar trim around Don's door. His grasp was awkward, but he was determined to get every last bug that might be hiding in the doorway.

We were fooled by the woodpecker's clues, and assumed the wood chips and damaged door meant a human intruder had attempted to break in. The red-crested bird wasn't trying to get in; instead, he was trying to get some tiny bugs out of Don's door for lunch.

Sometimes, we make these similar mistakes with what we assume about God.

Some of us think we know all there is to know about Him after reading a few verses from the Bible. Others assume God is just waiting for them to mess up so He can punish them. Many see Him as the God of Love, which He is, but choose to ignore that He is also the righteous judge.

These assumptions lead some to misunderstand the mission of Jesus, and they miss the message of God's love for them. When we focus on the state of the world or the cruel condemnation we receive from others, it's difficult to see beyond them to the cross, and to His miraculous resurrection.

A closer look at God's Word reveals that God didn't send Jesus to condemn us, but to save us. When we believe in the One who is the Way, the Truth, and the Life, He challenges us to be like His Son, who was motivated only by the will of His Father. God sent Jesus to do what He did because He loves us, and wanted us to know Him.

Bird Feeder:

"For God so loved the world that he gave his one and only Son, that whoever believes in him shall not perish but have eternal life. For God did not send his Son into the world to condemn the world, but to save the world through him." (John 3:16-17)

Birdbath:

"To the Jews who had believed him, Jesus said, 'If you hold to my teaching, you are really my disciples. Then you will know the truth, and the truth will set you free.'" (John 8:31–32)

Birdhouse:

"Jesus answered, "I am the way and the truth and the life. No one comes to the Father except through me."" (John 14:6)

For the Birds:

Hairy and red-headed woodpeckers will make their home in a house with a base that is 6" x 6" wide. The entrance hole needs to be 2" wide and 10" up from the bottom of the nest to give them plenty of room to raise their babies. If you see a lot activity in dead trees with hollowed out holes in your woods, it could be that these woodpeckers or others have nests there. Before cutting it down for firewood, make sure there isn't a new nest of young nestled into its safety. Dead wood is also an excellent food source for many birds, so if you leave a few standing, you are doing the birds a favor.

Aunt Goose

One spring day, while walking around the lake, I saw a family of Canada geese. The downy babies had no fear of me, so I was able to get close to them. I watched their sleeping parents and wondered why they didn't chase me away. Suddenly from behind me came a threatening hiss! The goslings headed for the protective wings of their parents, and I turned slowly around. A big, white farm goose stretched her neck and repeated her warning. I moved away.

From a safe distance, I watched the goose family and their imposing white guard. The birds had an understanding. The goose with no family of her own took charge of protecting this one. Like the Queen's Guard at Buckingham Palace, she paced the area, head raised, eyes always watching

A couple of weeks later, I returned to the lake. The white goose still kept her eyes on the now gawky goslings. When they wandered out of their invisible safety zone, their adopted Aunt Goose would let out a warning "Honk!" The young geese quickly returned to their parents.

Sometimes we are like the goslings, and we want to wander where we shouldn't. That's when, as believers, we can sense the call of the Holy Spirit, guiding us away from temptations and danger. His Spirit is also the One who walks with us when we're facing the things we fear the most.

Bird Feeder:

[Jesus said,] "'And I will ask the Father, and he will give you another Counselor [the Holy Spirit] to be with you forever'" (John 14:16)

Birdbath:

"May the God of hope fill you with all joy and peace as you trust in him, so that you may overflow with hope by the power of the Holy Spirit." (Romans 15:13)

Birdhouse:

"For the grace of God has appeared that offers salvation to all people." (Colossians 1:9-10)

For the Birds:

Old bread, including donuts, is never wasted if thrown to the geese. Sparrows, blackbirds, pheasants, quail, and ducks all enjoy these treats, too. Keep leftovers in the freezer. When the bag is full, head for a nearby lake or pond where geese are known to be.

After putting the treats out to be consumed, pull up a lawn chair and wait to see who comes to your wildlife smorgasbord first. If you have the time, take a camera, your journal, and a cup of coffee. You never know what God might have in store for you there.

Birth Announcement

One spring morning a wren fluttered around me at the bird feeders. "What do you want, little fellow?" I asked the persistent visitor. He flew back and forth, singing. I followed him to the wren house nestled into the grapevines growing up the arbor.

He waited for me on top of the house. Nothing in his actions showed fear or a need for help. He cocked his head and listened. The female joined him. From inside came the sounds of tiny baby wrens. I was hearing their first songs. Soon, Mama returned to the little ones, and Papa went in search of food.

Leaving their house in the vines, I smiled. The wrens seemed to be celebrating the birth of their babies. Could it be? Later that day they chased me away from their little house. Walking away, I felt little doubt about their earlier intentions—they had wanted to tell someone their good news.

Good news is worth singing about. God sent out announcements about the birth of Jesus centuries before His arrival and recorded them in the book of Isaiah. In time, He sent angels to tell others about the coming of His Son. The first angel came to a young virgin girl named Mary to announce His arrival into her womb, and later to her fiancé Joseph to reassure him that his bride-to-be had done nothing wrong. Nine months later, the angels brought the news to the shepherds.

Then God placed a bright star to lead the watching wise men to the Child, so they, too, could look upon the Savior who had been sent into the world.

God recorded several re-birth announcements in His Word reminding us of those who believed in Christ before us; the twelve disciples who later proclaimed His message to thousands, the broken woman He met at the well, the thief on the cross next to Him, and the man renamed Paul who met Him on the road to Damascus, are just a few.

God continues to announce how essential the birth of Jesus is, and as always extends the invitation to all who hear it, to believe and be saved—have you responded to yours yet?

Bird Feeder:

"Everyone who calls on the name of the Lord will be saved." (Romans 10:13)

Birdbath:

"In the same way, I tell you, there is rejoicing in the presence of the angels of God over one sinner who repents." (Luke 15:10)

Birdhouse:

"For it is by grace you have been saved, through faith—and this is not from yourselves, it is the gift of God— not by works, so that no one can boast." (Ephesians 2:8-9)

For the Birds:

A birdhouse box that has a 4" x 4" base with an entrance that is 7" up from the bottom of the nest will serve many species of birds. Chickadees and wrens will use a house with a 1⅛" entrance. Nuthatches and downy woodpeckers need an opening that is 1⅜". The tufted titmouse will nest in a box that has a 1¼" entrance. If you are trying to attract chickadees, nuthatches, or downy woodpeckers, line the houses with untreated wood chips or leave little piles of them around the area for the birds to find for themselves.

Call of the Wild

When I hear their distant calls to each other as they fly in formation over our home, I'm immediately ready for one of my favorite outings; a visit to the park to feed the giant Canada geese. I am exhilarated by their presence on all sides of me, even after fifty-plus years of visits to them. Their beauty amazes me, and for a moment, I sense the pleasure of becoming their "provider" worthy of their very temporary affection.

They gobble up my offerings of dried corn or day-old bread, and sometimes stale popcorn. Hundreds of geese crowd around my legs and demand attention. Mallards and pigeons scurry among the bigger birds, hoping for their share.

They honk, squabble, and bite each other in their push to get the most. Feathers and dust sometimes fly. I throw handfuls to the crowd then offer the brave ones in front a treat from my hand. After a while, I leave a pile for the ones too eager for my attention, and I move deeper into the crowd to reach the more timid birds.

Their graceful necks, spectacular markings, and downy feathers are close enough to touch. But if I reach beyond their boundaries, I'm sure to get a hiss. A bite or wing spanking is not uncommon if they feel threatened. These are wild birds, and we have a short peace agreement. I bring the treats; they allow me to interact with them.

When the food is gone, so are they. I am left alone with only a messy reminder of their presence, still on the bottom of my shoes. They enter the water, thirsty for a cool drink of water after their snack.

Every fall, I eagerly listen for this call of the wild, and anticipate once again being in their midst. Even now as I write this, I remember the feeling of their hard beaks bopping corn or bread out of my open palm.

Daily, I hear the Spirit of God calling me to join Him in His Word where He generously satisfies my spiritual hunger and thirst. As I enter my time with Him there, my appetite is sometimes similar to the geese—voracious, and I hear my inner voice demanding that He feed my starving soul. I beg, "Give me something from Your Word today, God!" He hears and answers my prayer, and I leave my time in His Word filled to the depths of my soul.

He will do the same for you.

Bird Feeder:

"Blessed are you who hunger now, for you will be satisfied." (Luke 6:21)

Birdbath:

"Let them give thanks to the LORD for his unfailing love and his wonderful deeds for mankind, for he satisfies the thirsty and fills the hungry with good things." (Psalm 107: 8-9)

Birdhouse:

"Your word is a lamp for my feet, a light on my path." (Psalm 119:105)

For the Birds:

It's fun to give the birds and animals a special treat any time you feel like celebrating—I'm not sure why, but sharing with them at these times, multiplies my joy. Dried fruits, nuts of all kinds, popcorn, crackers, bits of cookies, apple chunks, pretzels, any flavor bread, dog food, cracked corn, cereal, and sunflower seeds all attract guests to the holiday smorgasbord.

It's also easy to provide the birds with fresh water throughout the year by using birdbath heaters. Another way is to put out a pie tin with fresh water in it a couple of times a day. When I do this, by the time I shut the door, I have a visitor or two already enjoying a quick drink.

Cat's Meow!

I heard a yowling cat in the woods by our house. I checked the feeders because a couple of local felines sometimes stalked them, silently. I saw only birds. The meowing continued, so I entered the woods to search for what I was convinced must be a suffering animal. If I did find it, I hoped I could help it. The woods became silent. I stood still for a few moments, and the chatter began again except for the cat sounds.

A few days later I saw a slender, gray bird with a black cap on our deck. He opened his mouth and meowed! *Excuse me?* Then as he gained confidence, the yowling started. My elegant visitor was a Gray Catbird, and was the "cat" I had searched for. Instead of a hurting animal, I had been on the trail of an imitator. I called my husband to tell him about the "Great Pretender" sitting on the railing.

Now and then, I pretend too. I say I'm okay when I'm not. I deny hurt until it becomes anger. Or worse, I profess to trust God but secretly let anxiety govern my internal life. Sometimes I let fear replace peace.

Everything is fine, on the surface, but in an uproar in my soul.

We can try to pretend our faith is vibrant by saying all the right words, but others are not easily fooled, and God never is. True belief is verbal and active. Others can see and hear it in the way I treat other believers, love my enemies, and in the spirit in which I do good works. True religion is a transformational belief in Christ plus an authentic joy in doing good to and for others.

The catbird wasn't pretending to be something he wasn't—he was given the "cat-call" by His creator. However, seeing him reminded me, that sounding like a cat didn't make him a cat. It's the same with Christianity. When someone hears me say I'm a believer, but they can't see me living what I believe they will wonder if I'm an imposter. If they hear me say I'm okay when I'm not, they'll see a liar. If they hear me say one thing and do another, they will know I'm a hypocrite.

Bird Feeder:

"In the same way, let your light shine before others, that they may see your good deeds and glorify your Father in heaven." (Matthew 5:16)

Birdbath:

"For it is by grace you have been saved, through faith—and this is not from yourselves, it is the gift of God— not by works, so that no one can boast. For we are God's handiwork, created in Christ Jesus to do good works, which God prepared in advance for us to do." (Ephesians 2:8-10)

Birdhouse:

"If you are wise and understand God's ways, prove it by living an honorable life, doing good works with the humility that comes from wisdom." (James 3:13)

For the Birds:

Supplemental feeding helps birds survive, since many species lose 80 percent of their young the first year of life. Feeders provide hours of entertainment. An added benefit is that the birds catch many annoying bugs (swallows), and others aerate your yard (flickers).

Caw

The crows in our yard greet the sunrise with raucous calls. These big black birds are family oriented. Last year's brood helps raise the next batch of young before leaving to start their own families. They often nest in the same territory as their parents.

One spring I watched a crow family raise a strong-willed youngster. He refused to feed himself when his siblings did. Sitting on a branch near his family, he constantly squawked, "Caw—caw."

The others moved away while his parents called him to eat.

Finally, one of the birds would bring him a bite, but he was never satisfied. This went on for days. I called him Caw and prayed he would eat—it was the only way I was going to get any peace and quiet.

After a week of being intermittently coaxed and ignored, he joined his family on the ground, still demanding to be fed. There was nothing any of us could do—this was one stubborn bird. I watched Caw remain on the sidelines crying and begging for someone to take care of him. He annoyed me. I thought, *He is just like some people I know!* Conviction filled my soul, and I wondered, "Why is it so easy to slip into self-pity mode?"

Caw was always welcome at the feast, but he had wasted his time and energy grumbling. When his family was filled and ready to explore the woods and fields for treasures to store in their nests, he was still hungry and frustrated.

Finally, Caw stopped his noisy grumbling, pecked at a kernel of corn, and swallowed. The crows welcomed him with softer sounds and settled in around him for breakfast.

Watching the bird family reunion, I realized the danger in my grumbling: in my own internal noise-making, I might miss the voice of the Shepherd calling me into sweet fellowship with Him.

"Sorry, Lord," I whispered in prayer. "Teach me to be like Caw's siblings, looking after the others in the faith instead of looking for spiritual handouts." I asked Him to forgive me for selfish thoughts and to remind me of Caw the next time I feel like complaining from the sidelines.

Bird Feeder:

"My sheep listen to my voice; I know them, and they follow me. I give them eternal life, and they shall never perish; no one will snatch them out of my hand." (John 10:27-28)

Birdbath:

"Finally, brothers and sisters, rejoice! Strive for full restoration, encourage one another, be of one mind, live in peace. And the God of love and peace will be with you." (2 Corinthians 13:11)

Birdhouse:

"Do everything without grumbling or arguing, so that you may become blameless and pure, children of God without fault in a warped and crooked generation. Then you will shine among them like stars in the sky." (Philippians 2:14-15)

For the Birds:

Bushes that produce berries and seeds provide both food and protection for birds. We leave a few apples in each of the trees, and all winter long the blue jays, cardinals, and crows enjoy these frozen fruit treats.

Cedar Waxwings

Early morning walks on the trails near our home are usually peaceful. One morning the brambles and trees along the blacktop path were full of noise. On the branches were hundreds of tired cedar waxwings. I stopped, and several incoming birds landed by my shoulder at eye level. I could have touched the weary travelers. Their bodies and song surrounded me—I felt like I was in the woodland scene in Disney's *Sleeping Beauty*.

They feasted on the drying berries that hung in clusters on the bushes, and my presence was still welcome. I whispered to them, "Hello." The bird nearest me cocked his head and moved closer to me. Somehow he knew it was safe. Within minutes, a jogger came up behind us and the birds took flight. I could feel the air move from the sudden flutter of their wings. I stood still and waited, sensing that they might return. Then, just as I had anticipated, they settled in around me again.

Some cheeped, some ate, and some went to sleep. I was so close that I could see individual feathers on their taupe bodies. Soon their sounds stopped while, except for a few watch birds, the flock rested. I stood in their midst, enjoying the same peace they had found.

When it was time for me to head for home, I spoke again, "Goodbye, beautiful birds." Walking away, I whispered a prayer of thanksgiving for the quiet joy flooding my heart after this up close and somehow personal bird encounter. It was as if God told them they could trust me to be kind to them. I stopped on the path and looked back at the birds one last time, and stood amazed knowing that God is in all things—even the perfect timing of their arrival into my life that day.

Remembering my moments in their midst, a familiar gladness wells up in me, and quickly becomes a quiet, abiding delight.

Bird Feeder:

"Shout for joy to the LORD, all the earth. Worship the LORD with gladness; come before him with joyful songs." (Psalm 100:1-2)

Birdbath:

"Satisfy us in the morning with your unfailing love, that we may sing for joy and be glad all our days" (Psalm 90:14)

Birdhouse:

"How amazing are the deeds of the LORD! All who delight in him should ponder them. Everything he does reveals his glory and majesty. His righteousness never fails." (Psalm 111:2-3)

For the Birds:

As fall approaches, you may notice the birds at your feeders are hungrier. Many of them are preparing for migration and are intentionally preparing for their upcoming trip. This is an excellent time to put out extra suet and seed. Hummingbirds will consume more nectar at this time so keep your feeders full of fresh sugar-water.

Cha-peep!

Moving out of the city was a lonely time for me. I was used to busy streets and human voices. As I adjusted to the many changes, I was sometimes afraid, and discouraged. Longing for company in the woods, I bought bird books, binoculars, bird feeders and many varieties of seeds.

A few days later, the yard was full of song and bright yellow birds. One of the males caught my eye. He was bigger than the rest and willing to wait his turn to eat at the feeders full of thistle seeds. The others were usually settling in for the night when he was finally done feeding.

Early one morning he sat on the feeder pole and sang out, "Cha-peep!" I sang his song back to him. He moved closer and seemed to enjoy my company.

The next morning I wondered if he would answer me. "Cha-peep," I called to my new friend. Instantly, I heard him echo, "Cha-peep."

Each day I would call, and he would come. As spring became summer, a little female joined him at the feeders. Soon, two baby goldfinches came with them, and I watched as they taught their young to eat the tiny seeds.

As the number of my finch friends grew, so did my love for our secluded country home. The days flew and although not all goldfinches do, it was suddenly time for Cha-peep and his family to migrate to a warmer climate for the winter. He was gone, but so was my loneliness; God used my beautiful yellow friend to remind me we are never truly alone.

Bird Feeder:

"The LORD himself goes before you and will be with you; he will never leave you nor forsake you. Do not be afraid; do not be discouraged." (Deuteronomy 31:8)

Birdbath:

"And so I walk in the LORD's presence as I live here on earth!" (Psalm 116:9 NLT)

Birdhouse:

"And be sure of this: I am with you always, even to the end of the age." (Matthew 28:20b NLT)

For the Birds:

Feeders need occasional cleaning. A sponge on a wire is great for cleaning the liquid feeders.

Others can be sprayed with a garden hose and left to dry overnight. Be sure to refill them early the next morning. Jelly cups, often mounted on a pole, need a drop of dish soap and a small brush to scrub them. Always rinse thoroughly.

Chick & Dee

Two chickadees waited on one empty feeder while I filled the other. Their trust surprised me. Many of these little black-capped birds eat at our feeders, but none were as tame as these two. I called the little one Chick. A tiny tuft of feathers stuck out of the top of his head like a wayward cowlick. The bigger bird, named Dee, watched over the other one.

Even filling the birdbath didn't frighten them away. Chick and Dee always came together and seemed to enjoy each other's company. I often see arguments break out between the birds at our busy feeders as they fight over whose turn it is or who reached for the best seed first. Yet with all the activity, these two friends (or siblings) never squabbled over territory or food.

Sometimes the news seems full of stories of people fighting about something. Angry words fill the headlines and courtrooms. In an effort not to get "taken" we discover we are living with our internal dukes up. We see the results as road rage grows more common, so do stomach ulcers, headaches, and sore jaws.

Recalling the simple life of Chick and Dee, I am once again blessed by their relationship. The two flew in, ate, and then left together. They faced all the same dangers and concerns other chickadees face— yet they lived at peace with each other and all the birds around them at the feeders.

I've experienced a similar bond of peace when praying with friends. Over and over again, trials become testimonies. Chaos transitions into calm. Pride and anger evaporate, and battle lines are erased. Competitions turn into partnerships. The hurting are helped and the fallen picked up. Prayer requests that are impossible to us get answered by God.

With our hearts united in faith and prayer, the peace of God reigned in our hearts and in our friendships.

Bird Feeder:

"Two people are better off than one, for they can help each other succeed. If one person falls, the other can reach out and help. But someone who falls alone is in real trouble." (Ecclesiastes 4:9-10 NLT)

Birdbath:

"Again, I tell you that if two of you on earth agree about anything you ask for, it will be done for you by my Father in heaven. For where two or three come together in my name, there am I with them" (Matthew 18:19–20)

Birdhouse:

"Glorify the LORD with me; let us exalt his name together." (Psalm 34:3)

For the Birds:

Some birdbaths are too deep for certain birds that can drown in small amounts of water. If possible, have two birdbaths: one for the bigger birds and another with a flat rock in the center for smaller birds. They will instinctively choose the best one.

Church in the Badlands

My family stopped at a small motel nestled in the South Dakota Badlands. After a night of baseball-sized hail and rolling thunder, silence woke me at four o'clock Sunday morning. I got ready for the day while my family continued to sleep.

Outside, I sat on an old log and waited. Clutching my Bible in my hands, I knew there would soon be enough sunshine to read. A soft yellow band of light broke over the rugged hills, and a moment later, the sky was streaked with a wash of tangerine and lavender. The rhythmic sounds of the bugs were replaced when one lone meadowlark flew to a nearby fence post and opened his throat to the heavens. Immediately, others joined him and a few soft calls from the killdeer blended in.

Not able to withhold my feeling of adoration, I, too, stood and joined in whispering a few choruses of praise to the Lord. As the bright orb of the sun reached over the mountain tops, I sat down. Surrounded by the singing birds, I read God's Word. After a time of prayer, I returned to the room and my family, strengthened by my time with Him.

Rejoicing still fills my heart when I remember that beautiful morning God and I had church in the Badlands. The still small voice of the Lord was my call to worship. His Word was my sermon, the birds my choir—with a meadowlark as their worship leader. The rugged rocks formed my sanctuary, and an old log became my pew.

Packing up the car later, I looked at the old log, and thanked God that He is always ready to meet with us anytime, anywhere.

Bird Feeder:

"My voice shalt thou hear in the morning, O LORD; in the morning will I direct my prayer unto thee, and will look up" (Psalm 5:3 KJV)

Birdbath:

"Shout for joy to the LORD, all the earth. Worship the LORD with gladness; come before him with joyful songs." (Psalm 100:1)

Birdhouse:

"The LORD is my strength and my shield; my heart trusts in him, and he helps me. My heart leaps for joy, and with my song I praise him." (Psalm 28:7)

For the Birds:

Old boxes of cereal emptied on the ground will be cleaned up before your own breakfast is over. Squirrels, blue jays, and crows enjoy left-over popcorn.

City Park

Spending time in my parents' backyard never felt like I was in a suburb of a big city. Although things have changed for them as they've grow older, I love to remember how it was.

Sitting there was like relaxing in a small town park. Flowers and shrubs flourished everywhere. A bench, picnic table, and swing offered choices for seeing the yard from several angles. Different kinds of bird feeders lined their yard, hung in trees, and dangled from their clothesline pole.

Each year, hundreds of goldfinches chose this spot as their favorite dining place. The trees were sometimes so full of the finches, they looked as if they were laden with exotic yellow and black blossoms. In this homemade bird sanctuary, robins built nests, orioles taught their babies to eat grape jelly, chickadees flitted about the trees, cardinals raised their families, yellow-headed blackbirds trilled from the lilac bushes while blue jays warned the others if a cat or hawk invaded their territory.

Mom and Dad's dog, Tasha, is now gone, but she guarded the yard by listening for the alarm of the blue jay, and made sure neighborhood cats stayed on the other side of her fence. When the birds heard the blue jay's warning song, they moved to higher ground and watched. Tasha rushed into the yard like a bomber on a mission. With the enemy banished, Tasha made her way back to the house and the blue jay sounded the all clear. With their refuge again predator free, the birds filled it with song and the soft flutter of wings as they flocked back the feeders.

To those of us who believe, God's Word says He is our hiding place, our refuge, and our protector. Still, life is difficult and often brings us into circumstances that try our souls. The enemy is seeking opportunities to attack and at times we are vulnerable. Other times, God allows us to suffer. But all of these things are temporary. The One who is forever faithful, will keep His Word, and we who believe will dwell with Him in His house forever.

Bird Feeder:

"God is faithful, who has called you into fellowship with his Son, Jesus Christ our Lord." (1 Corinthians 1:9)

Birdbath:

"How priceless is your unfailing love, O God! People take refuge in the shadow of your wings." (Psalm 36:7)

Birdhouse:

"Surely your goodness and love will follow me all the days of my life, and I will dwell in the house of the LORD forever." (Psalm 23:6)

For the Birds:

Clean the birdbath frequently with a hard force of water from the garden hose. If moss or fungus begins to grow in it, use dish soap and swirl it around with a cleaning brush. About once a month, clean the birdbath with a small amount of bleach in warm water. Let it sit for a few minutes, then rinse it thoroughly before refilling.

Cleaning House

We put up a martin house in the yard and watched. Scout birds would be in the area soon, and we wanted them to tell the others in their flock that this would be a great place to raise their young.

One morning, bird song came out of the house and a dark bird flew in and out with nesting materials. We hurried out to greet the new neighbors. Grackles had moved in on one side and sparrows on the other. We could have been disappointed because we knew they were noisy and messy birds. Instead, we watched with fascination as they busily prepared the apartments for their young.

On a nearby wire sat a scout martin. He was too late.

For years the grackles and sparrows returned to our martin house to raise their babies. The house had a porch on both sides, and the two families sat on opposite sides undisturbed by the presence of the other.

In the spring the male and female grackle worked together raising their family. Mrs. G. sat inside and Mr. G. went hunting for food.

When he brought home a tasty tidbit, his mate traded unwanted litter from inside the nest for him to carry away. They were a hardworking team, and their babies lives depended on their diligent labor.

The sparrows lived a similar life on the other side of the house.

Each morning, the songs of tiny grackles and sparrows broke the stillness—the babies were hungry. The routine began again. Papa left the house and mama waited at the doorway. The privilege of being parents to their little broods brought huge responsibilities, but the grackles and sparrows didn't shirk their duty.

Our favorite time to watch the house was in the evening when Mr. G. and Mr. S. sat on their porches. Their babies were asleep under their mother's wings, their mates had finally stopped sending them on errands, and the two males enjoyed a quiet moment outside before the sunrise brought another busy day full of parental responsibilities. They'd earned it after a busy day of work.

While we watched, I thought about how Jesus said that all of us who are tired can come to Him and find rest. After a busy day, during an on-going struggle, when we're disappointed, discouraged, or depressed, His invitation is gentle and kind. I felt those ancient words beckon my soul.

I looked at my husband, Jon, who sat beside me on the patio, and noticed that he was enjoying the birds and the way the woods around us were slowly quieting down as much as me. After a long day, he too was resting in the beauty of the moment. When he looked at me and asked what I was thinking, I decided not to mention the projects ahead of us the next day and instead, I pointed at the birds, and told him, "You, and those two."

Bird Feeder:

"My soul is weary with sorrow; strengthen me according to your word." (Psalm 119:11)

Birdbath:

"Then Jesus said, 'Come to me, all of you who are weary and carry heavy burdens, and I will give you rest. Take my yoke upon you. Let me teach you, because I am humble and gentle at heart, and you will find rest for your souls.'" (Matthew 11:28-29 NLT)

Birdhouse:

"I will refresh the weary and satisfy the faint." (Jeremiah 31: 25)

For the Birds:

Empty birdhouses when the babies have left to make it ready for the next family. Unscrew one side of the house and clean out old nesting materials. If you don't want sparrows taking over your bluebird or martin houses, plug the entries until the preferred birds will be in the area again. Check your bird book for approximate arrival dates in your area.

Cleaning with a Cockatiel

For a while I earned money cleaning other people's houses. One of my clients had a pet cockatiel. He had a dusky gray body, yellow comb, and orange cheeks. At first I kept him in his cage, not wanting him to mess where I had cleaned. He'd watch me closely, and when I got close he'd move closer to me, and when I walked away he'd squawk as if he didn't want me to leave. I liked that about him.

Now and then his verbal requests for my attention were unsettling—he'd call to me the whole time I was there. Neither of us had any peace. One day I sat by his cage and said to him, "I really want to get along with you—I'm going to pray for a solution that will work for both of us."

His humans told me that he loved being with people and probably wanted to spend more time with me. I still didn't want bird surprises for the family to find, but I wanted to interact with him and the thought of holding him delighted me. I shared an idea I had with his family, they said I could try it, and to my amazement it worked. I put on a baseball cap and he perched on my head. (I didn't want any surprises in my hair, either.) While I dusted, mopped, and scrubbed bathrooms he contentedly stayed with me. He never complained or squawked at me again.

Cleaning demands the use of both hands, and with all my bending and walking around, it was up to him to keep his balance. He understood what I needed him to do immediately. Our partnership became so natural to both of us that he could sometimes anticipate my movements and I'd feel him getting ready for me to change positions. Our new partnership brought us both peace.

The only time he wanted nothing to do with me was when it was time to vacuum—then he gladly returned to his cage. He learned my routine; and as soon as I put my cleaning supplies away, before I even reached for the vacuum cleaner, he hopped down onto my shoulder. I offered him my finger as a perch and returned him to his cage after he'd rubbed his beak on my nose.

It took a little time for me to discover a peace plan that worked for my cockatiel friend and me. When I did, it took very little effort for us to get along and experience a peace we wouldn't have enjoyed otherwise.

I'm easily unsettled by relationships that are more "squawk" than peace. If my feelings are hurt, living in harmony with these people is difficult. Sometimes, even the best of intentions are ignored, rejected, or misunderstood. Honestly, giving up would be far easier than giving in and being nice— again. However, when I take God's Word seriously and try to live in harmony with others, something bigger happens in my soul; it makes no sense, but I'm able to care deeply and genuinely for them.

And the coolest thing of all is this: the desire to live in peace with them, the compassion and love for them that floods my soul, and does not come from me. All of this comes from God. If it was all up to me, the result would be far different.

Bird Feeder:

"If it is possible, as far as it depends on you, live at peace with everyone." (Romans 12:18)

Birdbath:

Get rid of all bitterness, rage and anger, brawling and slander, along with every form of malice. Be kind and compassionate to one another, forgiving each other, just as in Christ God forgave you." (Ephesians 4:31-32)

Birdhouse:

"Above all, love each other deeply, because love covers over a multitude of sins." (1 Peter 4:8)

For the Birds:

If you need to use pest killer pellets, place a small basket over a confined area with a rock on top of the basket. This will protect bug-eating birds from ingesting the poison.

Colorado Hummers

My first step onto the world's highest suspension bridge at the Royal Gorge in Colorado was hard to take. The drop to the river was 1,053 feet with rugged rocks on each side of it. The river below looked like a blue ribbon lying on the canyon floor. The dread increased when the bridge started to sway from the movement of other people crossing it. When I reached the far side, I was eager to sit down on solid ground again where benches lined the veranda. Once seated, I quickly forgot about my fear of high places when I saw dozens of hummingbirds sipping nectar at the feeders. Since they are often territorial, I was amazed to see so many hummers feeding together. Some sat together while others hovered and sipped.

The abundance of tourists did not frighten or distract them. When a person got in their way, they let out a short peep and swerved to miss them. Their masterful aeronautics saved them from many head-on collisions with humans seeking souvenirs and ice cream cones.

I sat, watching them, when one small bird buzzed by close enough to cause my hair to move from the currents of its flight. Another hovered near my shoulder, inspecting me closely. One brave hummer paused for a moment near my face, and we observed each other eye to eye. Several fed in peace at the feeder by my head.

Sitting among them, I looked at the bridge I had to cross again. Fear did its best to ruin the moment, then I realized God was whispering a tender lesson into my heart: to enjoy the sweet nectar provided for them, the little birds had to overcome their natural fear of humans, and share the space on the feeders with other hungry hummers. While the hummers buzzed and hovered around me I knew that the God who said He would never leave or forsake me would be with me on my return journey across the gorge. Trust replaced fear, making the rest of the journey far easier. I was able to immerse myself in the rugged beauty around me and worship the One who created it all more fully.

Those moments shared with the hummingbirds offer us all a glimpse of the relationship God wants each of us to experience with Him. One where we trust Him to the point that we can step away from our fears, and walk anywhere He leads us. All of us who believe in Him, can intentionally overcome the fears that nag at and weaken us, transforming them into joy.

When I took my first step back onto the bridge, I felt a strength that wasn't my own. He was with me and that was more than enough to get me safely to the other side. Knowing that filled me with unspeakable joy.

Bird Feeder:

"The LORD is my light and my salvation—whom shall I fear? The LORD is the stronghold of my life—of whom shall I be afraid?" (Psalm 27:1)

Birdbath:

"The LORD is my strength and my shield; my heart trusts in him, and he helps me. My heart leaps for joy, and with my song I praise him." (Psalm 28:7)

Birdhouse:

"I can do all this through him who gives me strength." (Philippians 4:13)

For the Birds:

Hummingbird and oriole feeders need fresh sugar water every few days. Mix one cup of sugar to four cups of water and bring the mixture just to the point of boiling to keep the sugar solution from spoiling. Turn the heat off as soon as it starts to boil so nutrients aren't destroyed. You can prepare extra and refrigerate it for a couple of days before serving it to the birds.

Dangerous Crossing

After returning home from a day of shopping, my friend and I spotted twelve tiny pheasants milling around in the middle of the road. I pulled the car over and we walked toward the babies, hoping to hustle them to a safer place. I was certain their mother was nearby, and was glad when we heard her call from the field. A couple of the little ones suddenly plopped down, choosing to enjoy the warmth of the blacktop and ignore her.

The road was normally busy and the young birds wouldn't stand a chance if someone came over the hill at the speed limit. We tried again to coax them toward the ditch while their mother persistently called out to them.

One little pheasant was so frightened and confused by our presence that he turned from the direction of his mother's call and headed the wrong way. With one step, I was able to encourage him back into the flock. Just as we reached the ditch near the field where the mother waited, a car zoomed by. The babies scurried into the tall grass, unaware of the danger they had narrowly missed.

There are times in life when it's easier to choose comfort over obedience. We're tired, afraid, or unwilling to listen to His wisdom and instead, we trust our own feelings. We're aware on a soul level that we're headed for trouble, but let what we feel over rule what we know.

God, in His tender mercy, brings the memory of the little pheasants to my mind when I'm tempted to let what I feel trump what He is telling me. The little birds equated the warmth of the asphalt with safety when in truth, they were in the middle of a dangerous crossing that could have cost them their lives. God used the mother's diligent calls and two women to guide them to true safety.

In our lives, God most often uses His Word and His Spirit to lead us safely where He wants us to go. It's up to us to listen and obey.

Bird Feeder:

"Your word is a lamp for my feet, a light on my path." (Psalm 119:115)

Birdbath:

"For the word of God is alive and active. Sharper than any double-edged sword, it penetrates even to dividing soul and spirit, joints and marrow; it judges the thoughts and attitudes of the heart." (Hebrews 4:12)

Birdhouse:

"May the God of hope fill you with all joy and peace as you trust in him, so that you may overflow with hope by the power of the Holy Spirit." (Romans 15:13)

For the Birds:

If there is room in your yard, birds will use a small brush pile. Some species (brown thrashers and others) will nest there, giving you the opportunity to watch some normally shy birds. In the winter, small birds, (juncos and others) also appreciate the shelter. It's also true that a large pile might draw critters you do not want in your yard, so it's wise to carefully consider where or if you want to provide this kind of environment for the wild ones in your neighborhood.

Dirt Bath

A wren landed on the railroad tie at the edge of my wildflower garden while I was weeding. I had dropped a small pile of dirt that was clumped to the roots of the weeds, and the warm sun had dried the soil to a powdery dust. It was just right for a little bird to enjoy a dirt bath. The wren watched me for a moment, decided I was no threat, and he dove in. Reveling in the warm dusty soil, he lost himself in the moment and fell off the tie onto the grass.

I couldn't help but laugh. With his feathers literally ruffled, he flew to the branch above my head and scolded me. I guess he thought it was my fault. Until that moment, I didn't know birds experienced embarrassment. He finally gave up his verbal tirade and sat and watched me.

"Silly bird!" I called to him.

I took a break from my work to contemplate the lesson of the wren. Sitting on my bench, I realized that sometimes, I behave just like the little bird with the big song. When I do something embarrassing, I'd rather blame someone or something else too. My internal defenses rise as pride tells me it can't be my fault. Shame shows up, and I can feel my cheeks redden.

If someone laughs before I have time to see the humor in it, anger joins pride, and I find myself wanting to scold that person for making my circumstance worse. When I have chosen not to hold my tongue, my embarrassment is multiplied.

Although I usually recover quickly, like the wren, I sulk for a bit because my blunders are not fun, even if they are funny. Eventually, a merciful relief floods my soul as I let God have His way with my feelings. I join in the laughter, pride retreats, my cheeks cool, and my embarrassment eases.

A few minutes after his fall from the dirt bath, the wren hopped to a branch closer to me. His humiliation and frustration were forgotten as he sat there singing with his whole body. It was as if he'd forgiven me. I went back to my weeding glad for his presence, and blessed by his jubilant solo.

Bird Feeder:

"When pride comes, then comes shame; but with the humble *is* wisdom." (Proverbs 11:2)

Birdbath:

"My dear brothers and sisters, take note of this: Everyone should be quick to listen, slow to speak and slow to become angry, because human anger does not produce the righteousness that God desires." (James 1:19-20)

Birdhouse:

"Sing and make music from your heart to the Lord. . ." (Ephesians 5:19b)

For the Birds:

Many birds like a dust bath to rid their bodies of parasites. You can make one for them by outlining a 3' x 3' area with attractive bricks or rocks. Fill the area with an equal mix of sand, loam, and sifted ash to give them a waterless bathing pool. Gravel driveways are also favorites for many birds.

Doing It Her Way

A wren industriously built a nest in the new house hanging from the apple tree in the front yard. He worked from dusk to dawn choosing the right materials and checking them over carefully before entering the house with them. When he was done the next day, he sat on top of the wooden abode, tipped his little head back, and filled the air with song.

Later, he brought home his mate to inspect their nest. I was shocked when she tore the whole thing apart and started over. Twigs and grass flew out of the house and landed on the ground or floated away on the breeze. She chattered at him, and he brought new supplies. She discarded most of them. If he tried to take a shortcut and bring her something she had dumped out, she threw it out again. She fluttered and sputtered at him all day.

Finally, she had what she wanted and built the nest her way. She moved in, and he sat silently on the rooftop. *What a stiff-necked bird,* I thought while feeling sorry for the stoic little male. It was her way or no way. Her stubborn, ungrateful heart caused her to miss the point of his thoughtfulness and careful search for the right materials that would make a good home. *I thought, She is acting just like me when Jon first built me this home in the country. Although Jon would gladly have made the changes I desired, I got my way by doing it myself.*

Her behavior wasn't a pretty sight. But it was the action of the male wren that spoke to my heart. He guarded her with intense passion night and day, seemingly undisturbed by her picky ways. He never gave up on her. As I watched the wren go happily about his work, he reminded me of Jon. I realized the female wren and I both had a good thing going.

The little birds and the realizations left me determined to love Jon the way he loves me.

Bird Feeder:

"Love is patient and kind. Love is not jealous or boastful or proud or rude. It does not demand its own way. It is not irritable, and it keeps no record of being wronged." (1 Corinthians 13:4 & 5 NLT)

Birdbath:

"Love never gives up, never loses faith, is always hopeful, and endures through every circumstance." (1 Corinthians 13:7)

Birdhouse:

"Do to others as you would like them to do to you." (Luke 6:31)

For the Birds:

Leave a small pile of nesting materials somewhere for your birds. Cut cotton string, colorful yarn, or baling twine into strips. Small bits of shiny metallic thread often catch the eye of a creative nester. Dog hair and human hair from a brush will add a soft lining to a nest. Add a handful of grass cuttings and small twigs to their building supplies. The pleasure of watching the birds inspect the pieces is well worth the little time it takes to gather supplies for them. Add to the pile when it dwindles. You can clean it up when you think they are through raising their young, but remember many birds raise two or three broods per year; they may need to repair their current nursery, or build a new nest.

You can hang these materials in a basket in a tree, put them in a flower pot on your patio, or my favorite; you can purchase an inexpensive wire sunflower feeder and hang it where the birds eat.

Feeding the Geese

The boy stood in the park surrounded by Canada geese. Clutched in his hand was a small bag of cheese curls. He smiled as he looked from the bag to the birds. I couldn't hear what he was saying, but I could see that he was talking to them as he fed the big geese his crispy orange treats one at a time.

The geese were noisy and pushy, clamoring for the boy's attention. At first glimpse it appeared the geese were in control, but closer inspection revealed the boy was definitely in charge of the cheese curl distribution.

Looking at the geese through thick lenses, he was careful to see that each goose received a treat. I marveled at his actions. I wondered if he was naturally that thoughtful, or if he knew something about the pain of being overlooked and left out.

He had walked into the park on legs enclosed in metal braces, his gait stiff and wobbly on the uneven ground. In his hurry to get to the geese, I was concerned he might tumble into their midst. His wise mother didn't hurry to his aid, and instead allowed her beloved child the independence many others might take for granted.

When he saw the geese on their way to him, he turned to her briefly with a big, beautiful smile on his face. No wonder she'd held herself back—that smile was worth her sacrifice.

Then, instead of holding onto his treat, he gave away every last cheese curl joyfully. When the bag was empty, the geese turned and waddled toward the lake. The boy walked to the swings over the uneven ground, his smile bigger than before. With one little bag of treats he had fed a gaggle of geese.

Life sometimes surrounds us with pressures and hurts. It would be easy to hang on to the few good things we have, hoping to satisfy our own discomfort, but this little stranger is a gentle reminder of the joy that comes from sharing what we have with others.

Bird Feeder:

"The generous will prosper; those who refresh others will themselves be refreshed." (Proverbs 11:25 NLT)

Birdbath:

"Little children, let us not love [merely] in theory or in speech but in deed and in truth [in practice and in sincerity]" (1 John 3:18 AMPLIFIED)

Birdhouse:

"Let us not become weary in doing good, for at the proper time we will reap a harvest if we do not give up." (Galatians 6:9)

For the Birds:

Wood duck houses often hold several wild families each year. When the wood ducks move out, woodpeckers and squirrels have been known to move right in. You can download a free wood duck house plan here:

http://www.woodducksociety.com/duckhouse.htm

Flicker

Every morning, soon after the alarm went off, we heard pounding on the roof for several days in a row. By the time we got outside to see who was up there, they were gone. We hoped one of the pileated woodpeckers wasn't beating on the roof because he might be strong enough to cause the roof to leak.

Finally, early one morning, I was outside when the banging started again. I looked up and saw a northern flicker fervently at work on our antenna. Jon, who was inside at the time, came out to get a look at the culprit on the roof and confirmed it was the same sound we had been hearing before. Outside it had a metallic sound, inside it was muffled.

Chasing the flicker away didn't work. In the end, we gave in to the flicker's persistence.

For weeks, the persistent bird came back every day. Finally, the flicker found what it was looking for and moved on; but until it did, we had to put up with the noise it created.

Jesus told us to be just like that flicker when we need answers from God. When He told His followers to *ask* God for what they wanted or needed, He used the Greek word *aiteo* (pronounced *ahee-teh'-o*), which means to "ask, beg, call for, crave, desire, require." This kind of asking is much like the tenacious flicker on our rooftop, who didn't stop pecking away at our antenna until his curiosity was completely satisfied.

The Word of God says in James 4:2, "You want something but don't get it. You kill and covet, but you cannot have what you want. You quarrel and fight. You do not have, because you do not ask God." Jesus promised God would answer those who *continue* to ask, saying in Matthew 7:9–11, "Which of you, if his son asks for bread, will give him a stone? Or if he asks for a fish, will give him a snake? If you, then, though you are evil, know how to give good gifts to your children, how much more will your Father in heaven give good gifts to those who ask him!"

Bird Feeder:

"The earnest prayer of a righteous person has great power and produces wonderful results." (James 5:16b)

Birdbath:

[Jesus said,] "Ask and it will be given to you; seek and you will find; knock and the door will be opened to you. For everyone who asks receives; he who seeks finds; and to him who knocks, the door will be opened" (Matthew 7:7–8)

Birdhouse:

"Let perseverance finish its work so that you may be mature and complete, not lacking anything." (James 1:4)

For the Birds:

Hanging bug catchers are annoying and can chase away birds. Swallows, wrens, and martins in your yard will help control flying insects. Flickers and robins will often take care of anthills and other crawling pests. When these natural helpers don't work, especially on large anthills, I put poison pellets out, under a large, small weave basket with a rock on it. That way birds and other animals aren't in danger of ingesting the poison.

Putting out bat houses will also mean fewer mosquitoes in your yard.

Here's a recipe for keeping gnats at a distance: (we use this same recipe for keeping bugs away from our apple trees!)

Gnat Be Gone

In a gallon bottle combine:

1 cup of sugar

1 cup of vinegar (we use white vinegar)

Fill the bottle half full of water

Add 1 banana peel

Hang this where children won't get into it and where the smell of fermentation won't bother you when enjoying time outside.

Another option:

In a small plastic container, place the following:

2 drops dishwashing soap (lemon scent seems to appeal to them)

1 tablespoon hot water

1/3 cup dark cider vinegar

And to lure them in, a piece of banana, apple, or sliced grape

Cover the container with plastic wrap and poke holes in the wrap with a pin. The gnats will drawn to the scent, and the smell won't be a problem for you. The scent doesn't bother me, so when I'm alone I don't cover the container.

Flying in Formation

In the spring and fall, giant Canada geese migrate through our area in streamlined Vs. Their honking fills the cool air. The lead bird slices the air to make flight easier for the birds directly behind him, and they do the same for the ones behind them.

The pattern has a purpose. Sometimes the front bird tires and falls back and a bird behind will move ahead. They share the responsibility of leadership throughout the journey. Birds with seniority in the family lead first. Age and marital status often decide where in the flock a goose is assigned a spot.

Order and precision are vital. Each bird gets his or her opportunity at just the right time. They fly at speeds up to seventy miles per hour for great distances with no mishaps or collisions.

The only time I ever saw them in chaos was when someone at the lake shot a gun. Thousands of geese tried to get in the air at the same time, but at first there was no designated leader. They collided with each other while trying to get away and frightened honks filled the air. Several birds were injured and fell to the ground. There, they walked around stunned, in pain, and confused.

This experience reminds me of people who suffer a catastrophe without Jesus. We naturally respond to sudden calamity with fear and anxiety. If we fail to take time listen to for the voice of our Shepherd, the result is chaos, noise, and fear that results in panic.

Like the frantic geese, we want to flee, but have no idea where to go.

Eventually, over the noise, the call of the leader birds could be heard. They were the first to recover, and they had chosen to retreat to the one place they felt immediately safe—the water. In the next few minutes, their flocks responded and landed near them. The lake was as full of geese as I've ever seen it. As the birds settled in, their honks changed to quiet, more assuring sounds as their fear receded, and peace returned to the park.

Bird Feeder:

"Do not be anxious about anything, but in every situation, by prayer and petition, with thanksgiving, present your requests to God. And the peace of God, which transcends all understanding, will guard your hearts and your minds in Christ Jesus." (Philippians 4:6-7)

Birdbath:

"My sheep listen to my voice; I know them, and they follow me. I give them eternal life, and they shall never perish; no one can snatch them out of my hand" (John 10:27–28)

Birdhouse:

"For God has not given us a spirit of fear, but of power and of love and of a sound mind." (2 Timothy 1:7 NKJV)

For the Birds:

At least eighty species of North American birds will eat beef suet, including many insect-eating birds that wouldn't normally come to the feeders. You can also purchase suet inexpensively wherever other bird food and supplies are sold. Most include nuts and fruit, which give the birds additional protein and energy for their trip.

My favorite suet recipe: (it's messy, but the birds love it!)

Suet Muffins

1.5 lbs of beef suet

1 large jar of chunky peanut butter

A mix of sunflower seeds, raisins, and corn—I don't measure—I just mix a little in.

Heat the suet on a low heat to melt, stir in the peanut butter and the other ingredients. I pour them into a six-cup muffin tin I use only for this project. As the mixture cools, it will "set." I then place each "muffin" in a plastic bag and freeze them.

If you want to make the pileated woodpeckers in your neighborhood happy, put a big lump of plain beef suet in a pie tin and let them have it just as it is. Other birds will join the party, but the big woodpeckers really enjoy this treat.

Foot Bath

A hard, pelting rain fell for days, and our yard showed the effects. Deep ruts spiraled their way through our grass, and rainwater filled them to the brim. The food in our dog Bandit's outside dish was soaked, so I threw it out into the yard. A few minutes later, an ambitious crow began to gobble down the sopping pellets. As he bounced around getting as many morsels as possible, the mud clung to his feet.

He became so laden with the slimy wet earth that he could barely walk, and flying was out of the question. He hopped clumsily onto the cement patio and began pecking away at his feet. Dirt clumps flew in all directions while he worked to get himself clean.

Then he returned to the yard to eat more of the soggy dog food. Within minutes, his mud-covered feet were hindering his progress again. He looked at his feet, the patio, and then a nearby puddle. This time he jumped into the puddle and soaked his feet until they were clean. Then he returned to finish his breakfast.

Smart fellow that he was, he repeated the cleansing process, always returning to his unexpected banquet burden-free.

When life is difficult, we feel like we are walking through a mud-filled bog, every step adding weight to our worry. We search the world in vain for solutions when the answer is as close to us as our hearts. We hear His voice, and we resist the relief and refreshment He offers.

As I watched the crow consider his options—patio or puddle—I thought about my pending problems. I could continue to wallow in the weak wisdom of the world, or I could embrace God's wisdom and experience freedom—even if my circumstances didn't change.

Like the intelligent bird, I made an intentional decision: I would listen to the One who has overcome the world. It's a choice I must repeat often, because life is full of problems, sorrows, and trouble. Each time, like the bogged-down bird, I must decide who I will turn to; the world or the One who made it.

Bird Feeder:

"I have told you all this so that you may have peace in me. Here on earth you will have many trials and sorrows. But take heart, because I have overcome the world." (John 16:33 NLT)

Birdbath:

"It is better to take refuge in the LORD than to trust in people." (Psalm 118:8)

Birdhouse:

"So if the Son sets you free, you will be free indeed." (John 8:36)

For the Birds:

A handful of dog food gives nourishment to larger birds such as crows and woodpeckers. . .and their young. It will also draw raccoons. If you prefer not to have these critters in your yard, feed the birds this high-protein treat during the day and make sure the leftovers (if there are any), are cleaned up.

Goldie

Bam! A bird flying into the window is an unhappy sound to bird lovers who keep feeders near their houses. We ran outside to see if the bird was alright. My husband and I found a female goldfinch lying on the lawn chair. Jon picked up the unconscious bird, and I encouraged him to gently rub her back. After a few strokes, she blinked and settled into a better position in his cupped hand.

Jon talked to her. She cocked her head to get a better look at him, and snuggled in. When he offered her a finger to perch on, she accepted. Looking around the woods and feeling safe, she roosted on his extended digit. A few minutes later, she flew to a nearby branch and preened her feathers.

When she was fully recuperated, she went to the feeder for a bite to eat. Looking at the woods and alternately eyeing the window, she finally flew off in the right direction.

Several days later, a female goldfinch stayed on the feeders while we moved around the deck. Her trust made me wonder if she was the one who had rested in Jon's hand. We called her Goldie.

Sometimes we fly head-on into a barrier we don't see coming. An unexpected discouragement or hurt can knock us for a spiritual loop. It is during these times that we can trust what God told Joshua when he was given the job Moses once held. Over and over the new leader was instructed, "Do not be afraid; do not be discouraged. . ." Reading this story again recently, I realized that continued fear and discouragement are choices I make. God is very clear—these are things you and I do not have to carry in our hearts.

Joshua took God at His word; the people entered the Promised Land, and the walls of Jericho came down. This testimony of what God did in and through Joshua, if we let it, can transform discouragement into purpose.

The little goldfinch in Jon's hand that day is a tender illustration of the power of a touch. For her, it was bird CPR. For us, learning from Joshua's testimony, we can choose faith over fear and the walls keeping us from God's purpose and promises, will crumble. And, like the psalmist, we will be able to say, "Though an army besiege me, my heart will not fear; though war break out against me, even then I will be confident." (See Psalm 27:3).

No matter what we face, when we believe in Jesus, we are His. Forever. (See John 10:27-28) Take this to heart: as Christians, we can choose to live with fearless confidence and strength.

Bird Feeder:

"Be strong and take heart, all you who hope in the LORD." Psalm 31:24

Birdbath:

"Then the Lord said to Joshua, 'Do not be afraid; do not be discouraged.'" (Joshua 8:1)

Birdhouse:

"Be on your guard; stand firm in the faith; be courageous; be strong." (1 Corinthians 16:13)

For the Birds:

Plain peanut butter is a high-protein treat for birds. Mix grit or cornmeal with it to keep it from sticking to the outside of a bird's beak. Another good way to serve this snack is to thin it with jelly. Birds love both.

Gone Fishing!

On a bridge near our former home, Jon and I used to observe American bald eagles from our car. Early one morning we watched as two adult eagles began their breathtaking dance of courtship. We drove away, giving them their privacy as dawn started to color the sky.

Another day I watched one of these great birds fish for his breakfast. He hovered in midair, watching the murky water below him; then with a sudden drop, he skimmed the water. He missed when a car with a loud muffler roared by and broke his concentration. Instead of returning to the river, he settled in a nearby tree, where he fluffed out his feathers, scanned the area, and looked at me. For a brief moment, we had eye contact.

Although I hadn't made the noise that messed up his fishing, I didn't want my presence to further disturb his dining experience, so I left. I knew when he felt like it was safe, he'd return his focus to the water below and accomplish one of the things he'd been created and equipped to do: fish.

While some distractions can be good—like when a friend encourages me to let housecleaning go another day so we can share some unexpected time together—other detours, should be ignored.

When I determine to do something God wants me to do, it is amazing how many interruptions try to gain my focus or excuses arise for me to do something else. These are usually loud, annoying, and give me a reason to sit on the sidelines in hesitation.

In those times, I'm learning to listen deeper for the still small voice that whispers His plan to my heart. Then I am able to shake off the urgent distractions and respond to Him. When my heart and mind are united in this listening place, I hear the voice of Wisdom with greater clarity.

When I fail to listen to God's Spirit, I end up exhausted, weak, ineffective, grumpy, and whiny. It feels like I'm walking through mud up to my knees and that there's a "short" somewhere in my personal electric system.

For most of us, distractions lead to chaos and results in a loss of focus and fatigue.

I think I might purchase a sign for my office that says, "Gone Fishing!" to remind me what I learned from the eagle about listening deeply. First, he found a safe perch on a sturdy, high branch. Then, he took time to scan the area, regrouping for his mission before diving right back in. I knew from past times I'd watched, that he would then refocus all his energy on the water below, and when it moved just so, or the sun captured the shiny gills of a fish, the eagle would succeed.

Bird Feeder:

In Proverbs 8:33-35 wisdom says, "Listen to my instruction and be wise; do not disregard it. Blessed are those who listen to me, watching daily at my doors, waiting at my doorway. For those who find me find life and receive favor from the LORD."

Birdbath:

". . .but those who hope in the LORD will renew their strength. They will soar on wings like eagles; they will run and not grow weary, they will walk and not be faint." (Isaiah 40:31)

Birdhouse:

"Whoever belongs to God hears what God says." (John 8:47a)

For the Birds:

One of the best places to watch eagle is in Wabasha, MN at The National Eagle Center. Visit their website to learn more.

http://www.nationaleaglecenter.org/

Goose Crossing

In Rochester, MN, if a Canada goose decides to cross the road, he has the right of way. The oncoming driver's first and only warning is when the goose first steps out onto the road. Several other geese usually follow the leader. They seem to know the law is on their side, and rarely hurry. Sometimes a second group, seeing the traffic is already stopped, will hurry and join the first.

Some drivers inch forward and separate the geese to get past them. The next driver may try to pass on through, but usually when the next goose steps off the curb, it is time to stop again. A blaring honk might move the birds to flight but usually only brings a look of disdain from the geese.

This slow mode of transportation, one webbed foot in front of the other, is how parent geese move their goslings that cannot fly to better feeding grounds or new places to rest. When the little ones cross, drivers rarely get angry. Babies bring out the best in us—even during rush hour.

Many of us find waiting difficult. We were in a busy restaurant recently, and everyone had their names on the list. The line went out the door and down the side walk. An older man got tired of seeing others seated before him, even though they'd arrived and checked in first. In an attempt to change his position on the list, he decided to take the young, and seemingly shy host to task. To the older man's surprise, the host showed him again where his name was, along with the time it had been recorded it, and told him that it was likely he and his family would be seated in less than ten minutes. The angry man grabbed his wife and granddaughter by the arms and shoved them towards the door grumbling about talking with the manager and complaining to the corporate office.

The host simply called the next name on the list. Waiting for our turn to be served was somehow much easier after the exit of the rude fellow. All his "honking" had not gotten him a seat and to those who knew him, he lost their respect.

Sometimes I'm pushy with God. Certain I've waited long enough I beg, and then demand that he answer my prayers now. My impatience doesn't move my request up on his list, I don't get better or more service from Him, and in the long run, I lose a little self-respect every time I throw one of these tantrums. This isn't approaching the throne of grace boldly or asking persistently like the widow in the parable (See Luke 18:1-7). This is me being a spoiled child who wants her way with the God of the universe. I know because of the awful way my soul feels, like tarnished silver that needs a good polishing.

Normally, with tears flowing, I utter a simple, "I'm sorry." As soon as those words leave my soul, it happens. My childish tirade is forgiven, and my soul has that shiny, just polished feel. Waiting becomes easier—much like when a mother goose steps off the curb with a gaggle of babies following.

Bird Feeder:

"Let all that I am wait quietly before God, for my hope is in him. He alone is my rock and my salvation, my fortress where I will not be shaken." (Psalm 62:5-6 NLT)

Birdbath:

"Yet the LORD longs to be gracious to you; therefore he will rise up to show you compassion. For the LORD is a God of justice. Blessed are all who wait for him!" (Isaiah 30:18)

Birdhouse:

"I remain confident of this: I will see the goodness of the LORD in the land of the living. Wait for the LORD; be strong and take heart and wait for the LORD." (Psalm 27:13-14)

For the Birds:

To keep ants away from hummingbird feeders and jelly feeders, smear petroleum jelly on the lower part of the pole. Since it melts in the heat, this must be replaced often. Or, at your local bird supply store or plant nursery, ask about "ant motes." They look like upside-down umbrellas, are usually inexpensive and easy to mount, and less work. Some of the new feeders, have ant motes built into the design. They are a little more expensive, ($15.99 to $20.99), but they work.

Great Blue Heron

I slid slowly into the ditch, hoping to get a closer glimpse of the great blue heron. Settling on a rock surrounded by cattails, I waited. A movement in the water caught my eye—and there he stood, watching the water below his spindly legs. In one swift move, the heron caught a fish, stretched his long neck upward, and swallowed. I wondered where the others were, since I had often seen several in this area.

When a semi-trailer went roaring by and backfired, I jumped. So did several herons that were hidden in the cattails around me. When they took off, I was close enough to see their brilliant blue under-feathers and feel the air ripple across my face from their movement.

I sat back down on the rock, my heart beating a faster rhythm.

Driving home, I realized the herons had let me enter their secret hiding place. My presence did not alarm them. I couldn't explain their behavior, so I accepted it as a gift from God. I grinned and declared out loud, "Thank You, Lord, for this special blessing today!"

Later, I thought about the big birds again, and how I was so involved in looking for them that I almost missed them. Surrounded by the birds, I was completely unaware of their presence, but they knew where I was.

Sometimes it's like this with God. We go where we think He'll be, we look, and we don't see Him. We're in the right place, with the right motives in our hearts, and still we almost miss Him. How can that be?

Many times it's because we miss the fact that, for believers, God is as close to us as our own hearts. The very Spirit of God dwells in us (See 1 John 4:15-16 and 2 Timothy 1:14). It's wonderful to go to church, and to retreats focused on God, and to quiet places to meet with Him, but we must remember that God is in these places because He is wherever we are.

If we're so focused on looking for God where we expect Him to be—in the distance—the way I was looking for the herons, we run the risk of overlooking Him. I saw one of the great birds out in the water, but nearly missed the many who were so close to me, that I could have touched them.

God is near. He is even closer than the herons in the cattails were to me. In his Word, James tells us, "Draw near to God, and He will draw near to you" (See James 4:8a). Dear believer—God is where you are. Yes, He is in the church, at the retreat, and in the quiet places—because you and I take Him there.

Bird Feeder:

"Do you not know that you are God's temple and that God's Spirit lives in you?" (1 Corinthians 3:16 NET)

Birdbath:

"Rejoice in the Lord always. Again I say, rejoice! Let everyone see your gentleness. The Lord is near! Do not be anxious about anything. Instead, in every situation, through prayer and petition with thanksgiving, tell your requests to God." (Philippians 4:4-6 NET)

Birdhouse:

"And if the Spirit of him who raised Jesus from the dead is living in you, he who raised Christ from the dead will also give life to your mortal bodies because of his Spirit who lives in you." (Romans 8:11)

For the Birds:

Every serious birder needs a good pair of binoculars. Prices range from $99 to $4,500, and many are offered through trade magazines for bird-watchers and camera stores. Read up on the options before selecting the pair that is right for you. If you know others who watch birds, ask them what binoculars they use, and if they live nearby if you can take a look at them. An excellent place to ask is at your local wild bird feed store or a local wild life center.

If you like to bird watch when you travel, size can be an important consideration.

Hidden Treasure

One morning, I heard an unusual noise outside at the dog food dish. To my surprise, a northern flicker was chasing hungry squirrels away from the bowl by pecking their heads with his beak. He obviously didn't want to share his treasure with anyone. The squirrels scrambled to get away, chirring an angry rebuttal. I watched the industrious bird smash a few nuggets of food on the cement and eat them. Then his day's work began.

He took a piece of dog food to a nearby tree and stashed it in the trunk. He worked until the dish was empty. Later, I inspected his work. Dog food was tucked in the bark, up and down the tree. Still on guard, the bird chased me away with a flutter of wings and an angry trill from his throat.

The next morning I watched the squirrels steal every carefully-placed morsel from the bark of the tree. By storing the food, the flicker accomplished a good work. Yet, all the bird's hard labor profited him nothing.

Watching the dog food disappear, I thought about my own work. Does what I do have eternal value, or is it unfruitful like the flicker's hidden treasure?

I reread the parable in Matthew 25:14–28 about the master who gave money to three of his servants, according to their abilities. Two of the servants doubled their funds by using it to trade with others and thus returned the increase to their master. The satisfied master then trusted them with even greater opportunities.

But the third servant, lacking faith in the master, hid the provision, fearing the consequences of failing and owing the master when he returned. Angered by the servant's laziness, the master told the third servant to give his money to the first, who knew how to use it for doing good and was determined to do good for the master.

We are instructed by God in 1 Timothy 6:17 not to put our hope in wealth, "which is so uncertain," but to put our hope in God, "who richly provides us with everything for our enjoyment."

Thinking about the flicker's "buried" provisions, I again reconsidered the tasks that so often fill my days. As I searched my heart for answers, I asked God, the Master of my heart, to help me understand how to use all I've been given (money, abilities, and time) for Him. This was the beginning of a new adventure in my walk with God. He led me deeper into His Word and into the listening side of prayer. The more time I spent with Him, the more my soul yearned for Christ-like wisdom, and the desire to be rich in good deeds grew. God tells those of us who believe in James 1:5, "If any of you lacks wisdom, you should ask God, who gives generously to all without finding fault, and it will be given to you."

I asked, and He continues to answer. He will do the same for you.

Bird Feeder:

"In him [Christ] lie hidden all the treasures of wisdom and knowledge." (Colossians 2:3 NLT)

Birdbath:

"Command them to do good, to be rich in good deeds, and to be generous and willing to share. In this way they will lay up treasure for themselves as a firm foundation for the coming age, so that they may take hold of the life that is truly life." (1 Timothy 6:18–19)

Birdhouse:

"Cry out for insight, and ask for understanding. Search for them as you would for silver; seek them like hidden treasures." (Proverbs 2:3-4)

For the Birds:

Apples and oranges delight a host of birds, including flickers, robins, and orioles. Even if they seem too old for human consumption, they're still good for birds and other wildlife. We leave a few apples at the tops of our trees and all winter long the squirrels, blue jays, and crows enjoy a sweet, frozen treat.

House Beautiful

My friend always put a lovely wreath on her front door. One year she used silk flowers with a flowing raffia bow. It was beautiful and reminded me of one I'd seen in a glossy magazine. Early one morning she heard someone at the door. She looked out, but no one was there. Walking away, she heard the sound again. Stealth seemed to be a good idea, so she went out the side door and peeked around the corner.

A female robin was busy building a nest in the curve of the wreath. Checking on her new tenant the next morning, Kathie was amazed at the bird's handiwork. The robin had artfully used the raffia ribbon in her construction. The straw was woven in and out in graceful waves along the outside of a mud cup. The nest was so intricately attached to the wreath, it was now part of it—there was no way to see where one ended and the other started. Not wanting to injure the little birds growing inside the eggs, my friend invited me inside for coffee and to brainstorm ideas.

After awhile, I watched her write a few words in beautiful script across a large piece of paper. Then, with the tenderness and understanding of a mother, she pasted the note on the door that read, "Shhh, babies sleeping! Please use the side door."

I walked home thankful the bird had chosen a place where the woman inside could be trusted.

From a nearby window, Kathie watched the robin raise her young. Both my friend and the mother robin benefited from the bird's choice to attach her nest to this door; my friend offered the bird family refuge and protection. The birds gave her wreath life and song.

When I am troubled for any reason, this story reminds me gently that I can trust God to be my refuge and protection.

Birdfeeder:

"But let all who take refuge in you be glad; let them ever sing for joy. Spread your protection over them, that those who love your name may rejoice in you." (Psalm 5:11)

Birdbath:

"Trust in him at all times, you people; pour out your hearts to him, for God is our refuge."

(Psalm 62:8)

Birdhouse:

"But I will sing of your strength, in the morning I will sing of your love; for you are my fortress, my refuge in times of trouble." (Psalm 69:16)

For the Birds:

Purple and house finches (sparrows, too) will often nest in expensive hanging potted plants. Sometimes this damages or kills the plant. An easy solution is to hang a silk plant early in the season somewhere you can keep it up until the babies have grown and gone. They might choose this site early and leave your more expensive plants alone. (However, this is not a guarantee!)

Hummingbird in the Mist

The yard was dry from the brutality of the drought. Cracks were beginning to form in the hard soil, and our grass needed a drink. The faucet squeaked as I turned on the soaker hose, and a gentle mist began to moisten the parched yard.

Sitting nearby with a glass of iced tea, I watched the goldfinches and chickadees at the feeders in the unrelenting sunshine. A huge bumblebee bumped into my cheek, backed up, then moved on, buzzing by my ear but missing me the second time.

Droplets of water fastened themselves to our dog cable and glistened in the sunlight. I heard a hum again and turned my head. With fascination, I watched as a hummingbird playfully refreshed himself in the mist from the garden sprinkler.

Then he landed on the cable and let the gentle spray of water wash over him as he worked his beak over his shimmering emerald feathers. His little head was soaked, and his tiny feathers stood straight up, making him look like he had a crew cut. Shaking off, he hovered out of range of the water as if to air dry his small body. Then he nourished himself with the nectar in a nearby feeder.

Seasons without hope can make our hearts feel parched and thirsty. We get stuck in the land of sadness, anxiety, and disappointment. Our hearts long for help, and sometimes we don't recognize that our longing is for God. Instead of looking to Him, we try out quick fixes crafted by human minds. These may bring temporary feelings of relief, but they cannot satisfy our thirst or refresh our parched souls the way Jesus can.

The time I spend reading the Bible, praying, listening to His Spirit, and trusting Him, are where God gently mists the parched places nothing else can reach. Like the hummingbird, I leave this tender soaking renewed in my mind, body, and spirit.

Bird Feeder:

"Hope deferred makes the heart sick, but a longing fulfilled is a tree of life." (Proverbs 13:12)

Birdbath:

"Create in me a pure heart, O God, and renew a steadfast spirit within me." (Psalm 51:10)

Birdhouse:

"Let us draw near to God with a sincere heart in full assurance of faith, having our hearts sprinkled to cleanse us from a guilty conscience and having our bodies washed with pure water. Let us hold unswervingly to the hope we profess, for he who promised is faithful." (Hebrews 10:22–23)

For the Birds:

Birds are attracted to running water. If you don't
have a fountain birdbath, another good choice is a
misting or soaker hose. Turn the water on to a gentle
flow in the morning or late afternoon, and then enjoy
watching as several kinds of birds play and bathe in
the soft mist.

In the Still of the Night

When I was a child, my mom listened to my prayers, tucked me in with a kiss, and turned out the lights. After she left, I listened to the night sounds through the nearby window as I tried to fall asleep.

Many nights in the tall pine tree outside my window an owl seemed to ask, "Whooo?"

When I heard him, I wiggled out from under the covers and knelt at the windowsill to look into the darkness. Between the branches, I could see the stars twinkling in the night, and the silhouette of the owl. I knew heaven was somewhere behind those stars.

I liked to leave the shade up because when the moon was high in the sky, it was a great nightlight. Looking into the ebony sky full of stars, I wondered if God could see me peeking out my window. I scanned the pine branches for the owl, hoping to see his silhouette in the tree.

Listening to his night song, I wondered if he was asking who could hear him singing in the night. Again, the owl gently called, "Whooo?"

"Me!" I whispered to him. Tired and with very cold feet, I finally climbed back under my covers, comforted by the owl's gentle song.

I had learned in Sunday school that God created everything. As my eyes began to droop in sleepiness, I found comfort knowing that included me, the stars, and the big bird in the evergreen branches, who sang to me in the still of the night.

Now, evening still brings the calls of the owl in our woods. Many nights find me barefooted and looking into the vast night sky, hoping to catch a glimpse of this nocturnal bird. The stars continue to twinkle from where God placed them to light up the night—and it is good.

In those sweet nights of my childhood, I was just becoming aware of the awesome presence of God in my life. In all the years between then and now, He has shown me His closeness through His creation. Even in times of crisis or when my heart has been shattered, God has revealed His presence and His mercy to me through a bird, flower, or wild creature. Every time. All I had to do was look. And, I take comfort in Psalm 34:18, which says, "The LORD is close to the brokenhearted and saves those who are crushed in spirit."

I understand what David may have felt when he wrote of God in Psalm 16:11, "You have made known to me the path of life; you will fill me with joy in your presence, with eternal pleasures at your right hand."

Now when I hear the owl calling, I whisper, "Good evening, God—it's me again." Then, silently, as the evening air embraces me, I worship Him in the still of the night.

Bird Feeder:

"On my bed I remember you; I think of you through the watches of the night. Because you are my help, I sing in the shadow of your wings." (Psalm 63:6-7)

Birdbath:

"At midnight I will rise to give thanks to You because of Your righteous ordinances." (Psalm 119:62 AMPLIFIED)

Birdhouse:

"Praise be to the God and Father of our Lord Jesus Christ, the Father of compassion and the God of all comfort, who comforts us in all our troubles, so that we can comfort those in any trouble with the comfort we ourselves receive from God. For just as we share abundantly in the sufferings of Christ, so also our comfort abounds through Christ." (2 Corinthians 1:3-5)

For the Birds:

Owls will nest in an open-ended box mounted at a 45° angle about 10' to 30' up from the ground. Make the base 9" square and drill holes in the bottom to let moisture drain out. Make two sides that are 9" x 30", a base that is 10½" x 30", and a roof that is 10½" by 36". The extra length provides an overhang to protect the opening from rain. Drill five holes in a 2¾" x 27½" mounting batten: three to screw the batten to the house at a 45° angle, with the two holes at each end attaching the box to the tree. Spread sawdust or peat in the bottom of the nest to create an inviting cavity for owls to raise their young. There are many places you can purchase owl houses, and here's a link to get you started:

http://www.wildbeaks.com/product-p/se519.htm?gclid=CKScyN6PvrYCFc9AMgodSlAA0w

Is It Spring Yet?

Each year the sweet southern breezes melt winter away. Creation announces the season change as the trees bud and the crocuses and tulips break through the ground. For me, it is spring when all the birds come home.

My spring vigil begins with the robins. They often return to Minnesota just before the last "spring snowfall," and about the time that the juncos are forming migration flocks. I watch as the goldfinches that braved our cold temperatures molt their winter brown feathers, and turn bright yellow. Large flocks of white swans fly north over head, calling loudly to each other during their long journey. Then the orioles, warblers, hummingbirds, cedar waxwings, indigo buntings, bluebirds, purple martins, tree swallows, and scarlet tanagers return. White pelicans rest on the nearby lake while on their long migration north. I scan the marshlands for the egrets and finally, the great blue herons.

As I watch the return of the birds, each arrival is a comfort to me that the seasons will continue just as God promised. Genesis 8:22 says, "As long as the earth endures, seedtime and harvest, cold and heat, summer and winter, day and night will never cease." And with each season, God speaks to us through the changes in the earth, and the creatures that fill it.

The migration of the birds, and eventually the butterflies amazes me. They fly long, hard distances, driven by strong internal instincts. Without maps or

GPS, they know when to start and where to stop. This "knowing" is hardwired into their DNA—we may not know how yet, but it is there, and most of them listen to it.

Winter can seem long in Minnesota and every year someone sarcastically asks, "Is it spring yet?" I answer in my head, "Almost—I haven't seen an oriole or a hummingbird yet. . .but I know they're on their way."

And when they get here, I will see the stars, moon, and sun with renewed clarity. The daytime sky will be a spring blue and the winds will be warm. As I watch and listen to this seasonal change, it always feels like the whole universe is gearing up for a party.

Even when my current circumstances are difficult, the song of the birds, the hum of the bees in the apple blossoms, the warming breeze, cleansing rains, and the woods transition from bare and brown to green, ignite a celebration of praise in my soul. Then it happens: creation and I rejoice.

Bird Feeder:

"Praise him, sun and moon; praise him, all you shining stars. Praise him, you highest heavens and you waters above the skies. Let them praise the name of the LORD, for at his command they were created. . ." (Psalm 148:3-5a)

"Praise the LORD from the earth, you great sea creatures and all ocean depths, lightning and hail, snow and clouds, stormy winds that do his bidding, you mountains and all hills, fruit trees and all cedars, wild animals and all cattle, small creatures and flying birds. . ." (Psalm 148:7-10a)

Birdbath:

"Let the heavens rejoice, let the earth be glad; let the sea resound, and all that is in it. Let the fields be jubilant, and everything in them; let all the trees of the forest sing for joy." (Psalm 96:11-12)

Bird House:

"For God is the King of all the earth; sing to him a psalm of praise." (Psalm 47:7)

For the Birds:

Some birds, like brown-headed cowbirds, sparrows, mourning doves, juncos, and others prefer feeding on the ground. I intentionally scatter some seed at the base of the feeders for them. Because I use the new "garden or deck" mixes, I have very few seeds sprouting. Another idea for these ground feeders is to put some seed in metal pie pans.

Letting Go

Fearless was the first raccoon we rescued and released. He came to us as an orphaned baby needing food, shelter, and love. At three years old, he began to reject us. Becoming aggressive and pacing his kennel, he snarled at us and no longer reached up to be held. He let us know that it was time to return him to his natural habitat.

We knew that keeping him in captivity would be wrong, and that we'd all be unhappy. No matter what, we had to do the right thing. It would take courage, but I knew the Lord would give us what we needed. Besides, we loved the little guy, and setting him free was our motivation from the first day he came to us.

I called the Department of Natural Resources and received permission to release him. The man on the phone told me about a place in the backwaters of the Mississippi River about ninety minutes away from where lived that we could take him deep into the woods beside a small stream and set him free.

With Fearless in the pet carrier, we thrashed through nettles and weeds more than six feet tall. The thick underbrush tripped us. Huge trees seemed to stand watch as we entered deeper into the forest. The stream bubbled over rocks, and a downed tree rested across the water. Birdsong surrounded us in the deep, thick woods. We heard duck calls and saw small fish in the glistening stream. Raspberry bushes

were in full bloom. This was the right place—a
raccoon's paradise.

We watched him as he peeked out of the carrier and
took his first steps into freedom. He sniffed the air
and touched the water before venturing into it, and
then he paddled and floated on the gentle current
immediately. Climbing a tree was easy for him,
though coming down was a bit harder.

Fearless did all the things a wild raccoon should: He
swam, ate minnows from the stream and crunchy
things from under rocks, and climbed to safety. We
watched him for at least thirty minutes, confident
that he would make it on his own. After looking at us
one more time as if to say "good-bye," he
disappeared in the tall weeds. We never saw him
again. Turning to leave, I asked God to protect him.
Tears poured down our cheeks—we were going to
miss him greatly.

A soft whooshing sound got my attention. A great
blue heron settled onto the small log and blinked his
eye at me. He was close, less than four feet away
from me, and fully aware of my presence. He
blinked once more and then gazed into the water.

It was time for us to go, time for Fearless to be free,
and time for the heron to fish for his lunch.

Following the stream out of the woods, we came to
where spring water flowed out from behind a rock.
Splashing in and out of its gentle flow was an indigo
bunting, scarlet tanager, and a yellow warbler. I

walked up to the natural fountain and put my hands in the cold water while the birds darted in and out around me, unafraid.

The release wasn't easy, but I walked away at peace in my heart because we had done the best we could for a little raccoon we loved so much. As we made our way back to the car through the thick brambles, I was comforted by the birds that God sent to welcome Fearless to his new home. Now he could be the raccoon God created him to be in the wild, and we were privileged to be his pit-stop on the way to freedom.

Bird Feeder:

"Remember, it is sin to know what you ought to do and then not do it." (James 4:17 NLT)

Birdbath:

"For every beast of the forest is Mine, *and* the cattle upon a thousand hills *or* upon the mountains where thousands are. I know *and* am acquainted with all the birds of the mountains, and the wild animals of the field are Mine *and* are with Me, in My mind." (Psalm 50:10–11 AMPLIFIED)

Birdhouse:

"Be on your guard; stand firm in the faith; be courageous; be strong. Do everything in love."

(1 Corinthians 16: 13-14)

For the Birds:

If you enjoy watching raccoons, possums, and other wild animals, but want to keep them from eating all your seed, leave leftovers for them. They love old bread, muffins, cookies, stale cereal, pasta—almost everything. Meat products attract flies and should only be left when you know it will be eaten that night. You will witness wild, even vicious disagreements, but you may also enjoy the beauty of wild parents feeding and teaching their young.

Love Song

One spring I heard a lovely song in the woods. The sweet melody came from high in an ironwood tree. I searched the budding branches for the source of the singer. The only bird in the tree was a feisty blue jay that seemed to find my presence a nuisance. He squawked and I moved a few feet away, hoping the other bird would start singing again.

Sitting at the picnic table, I waited. In a few moments, the melodious song resounded from the limbs of the same tree. I was certain the only bird there was that noisy old jay. Then I saw him open his mouth in song and release lovely sounds from his throat. Delight followed my surprise. He was pouring on the charm, hoping some lady jay would appreciate his love song. Throughout the day, he kept the serenade soft and romantic.

When I saw another bird fly to him later that day, I grinned with hopes that the flirty bird had found his mate. That evening their coarse, raspy calls filled the air as they conversed—so much for the gentle wooing earlier in the day.

Isn't that just like romance? At first, we put on our best clothes, smile, and attitude. We draw the one we love in by our wooing; we put effort into listening and caring. Then as we take each other for granted, our love song becomes rusty from a lack of use.

God never stops drawing us to a relationship with Him. He loves us so much that He sent His only begotten Son to save us. And His Son, Jesus, loved us so much that He let His enemies mock Him, spit on Him, and even beat Him, yet He still gave Himself as a sacrifice for the sins that kept them, and us from knowing God as our Father. Then, on the cross, He prayed for them. (See Luke 23:34)

God's Word testifies that Jesus is patient, kind, is never boastful, proud, rude, or self-seeking. He is not easily angered and when we believe in Him, He keeps no record of our wrongs. He never delights in evil but always rejoices with the truth. He protects, trusts, hopes, and perseveres for us—always. His love is the perfect demonstration of 1 Corinthians 13:4-13.

As I ponder this passage I am again convicted by these questions: if all of us who believe in Jesus were to love the way He did and does, would the world respond differently to Him? Would they also believe?

And finally, the question gets more personal: Does my song to the world sound like the grumpy jay or the One singing a melody of love?

Bird Feeder:

"So now I am giving you a new commandment: Love each other. Just as I have loved you, you should love each other. Your love for one another will prove to the world that you are my disciples." (John 13:34-35 NLT)

"Don't just pretend to love others. Really love them. Hate what is wrong. Hold tightly to what is good. Love each other with genuine affection, and take delight in honoring each other." (Romans 12:-10 NLT)

Birdbath:

"Three things will last forever—faith, hope, and love—and the greatest of these is love." (1 Corinthians 13:13 NLT)

Birdhouse:

"I pray that from his glorious, unlimited resources he will empower you with inner strength through his Spirit. Then Christ will make his home in your hearts as you trust in him. Your roots will grow down into God's love and keep you strong. And may you have the power to understand, as all God's people should, how wide, how long, how high, and how deep his love is." (Ephesians 3:16-18)

For the Birds:

Birdseed can spoil or become infested with moths. If possible, keep surplus seed in the freezer. The frozen food thaws quickly for the birds' consumption and the freezing keeps it fresh.

Making Mud

Spring budded everywhere. Lilac bushes burst open, the warm breeze whispered hope to my heart, tulips pushed through the hard ground, and the robins were back. However, no rain came, and it looked like another year of drought. I knew I was going to need to water my thirsty blossoms and fill the birdbaths.

Tired birds of all kinds came for the fresh water. From my kitchen window, I watched a young female robin begin building her nest. She needed mud to cement the sticks together that she gathered together for their nest.

So, this industrious bird flew to the birdbath and gathered a tiny bit of water in her mouth. From there she flew to a bare piece of ground on the edge of the lawn. She pounded the water into the hard dirt with her beak. She then used that tiny bit of mud to cement one twig to another.

Her labors and the remaining task before her overwhelmed my heart. After watching her make a few more trips, I helped her out. I turned the garden hose on and made a little puddle in the dirt for her. I also cleaned and refilled the now muddy birdbath.

Back in the kitchen, I peeked out to see if she understood the opportunity before her. She tipped her head back and belted out a sweet note of song before returning to her task using the puddle as her new source of mud.

By the end of the day, her nest was complete, finished off with a long piece of orange ribbon she found somewhere. Her simple decoration blew gracefully in the gentle breeze. Now she could focus on the upcoming arrival of her young.

Not long after, I found two tiny pieces of aqua eggshells on the ground under the branch where her home was securely anchored, and heard her babies peeping from the safety of the nest. Quiet satisfaction stole into my heart as I thanked God for letting me help their mother build the home they were nestled into.

Most of us believe in doing good for others, but putting that belief into action takes time and energy—something we are often lacking. We're busy. We work, pray, give, volunteer, raise money for great causes, and go on short term mission trips, but a question nags at our hearts: "What if I'm not doing enough?" We worry because the majority of the hungry are still unfed, the homeless are without beds, the orphaned and widows continue to hurt, and the prisons are full of people who need Jesus. (See James 1:27)

Dear believer—take heart! When we work, pray, give, and do motivated by who He is, and by His Spirit at work in us, He shines into the world through us. More gets done than we can see. Lives are changed, hearts are transformed, and hurts are healed. We can take comfort knowing that we have done what we were created to do: good works. While we can't do enough to relieve the whole world, we can rest knowing that it is enough to do our part. We can trust God to do what we cannot and were not called to do. The rest is up to Him.

And like the day I helped the mother robin make mud, we can enjoy doing good—even in small ways that will not be noticed by others, but are always seen by God.

Bird Feeder:

"Trust in the LORD and do good; dwell in the land and enjoy safe pasture. Take delight in the LORD, and he will give you the desires of your heart." (Psalm 37:3-4)

Birdbath:

"For we are God's handiwork, created in Christ Jesus to do good works, which God prepared in advance for us to do." (Ephesians 2:10)

Birdhouse:

"Neither do people light a lamp and put it under a bowl. Instead they put it on its stand, and it gives light to everyone in the house. In the same way, let your light shine before others, that they may see your good deeds and glorify your Father in heaven." (Matthew 5:15-16)

For the Birds:

While watering flowers, rinse the outside of liquid
feeders daily with the garden hose to keep the sugary
water from attracting bees and wasps. The sting of a
wasp or hornet can kill a hummingbird. Other birds
that stop for a drink, and will sometimes help the
hummers out. Downy woodpeckers drink sugar
water and don't mind chasing away the wasps and
hornets.

"Morning" Doves

Grandma and I sat on the steps outside her apartment before starting my lesson for the day. She was teaching me to sweep the sidewalk, something she did most mornings because a clean walk was important to welcoming her piano students and any neighbor who might stop by. The soft song of the brown doves resting on the telephone wires floated in the morning air. The sound comforted me. Grandpa was gone, and the grown-ups in my life told me heaven welcomed him. That might work for them, but my nine-year-old heart only knew I missed him, and it hurt.

"Grandma, what kind of birds are those?" I asked.

"Mourning doves," she replied.

"Because they sing in the morning?" I asked.

Grandma smiled, "No, child, they get their name from their sad song."

Dissatisfied with her answer, I asked, "Grandma, I like their songs. Can I call them the *morning* doves?"

"Yes," she agreed. For a moment, the sadness in her eyes lifted as the corners of her mouth did the same.

As a child, it was not difficult for me to believe that Grandpa was in heaven, because even though I didn't fully know who God was, I knew my grandpa loved Him and was loved by Him. I'd spent many hours in his rocking chair with him. He read from his Bible to me about Noah, Daniel, and Jesus. I watched his long fingers caress the thin pages with love and reverence. Because my grandpa believed in Him so deeply, I knew they were together.

In the fresh air of that morning, what was hard for me to believe was that the doves were sad when their songs sounded friendly with a touch of quiet joy. My heart ached, but the melody they sang offered something I couldn't explain then, but now know as sweet consolation.

All these years later, the fluttering of the dove's wings soothes my heart, although they sound like hinges in need a little oil. They come early and stay late, ushering in the morning, and the evening out with their song. Their arrival reminds me of the two, so long gone now, who let me see their love, joy, peace, goodness, and faithfulness. What I saw in them, led me to belief in Him much later.

Bird Feeder:

"But the fruit of the Spirit is love, joy, peace, forbearance, kindness, goodness, faithfulness, gentleness and self-control. Against such things there is no law." (Galatians 5:22)

Birdbath:

"The whole earth is filled with awe at your wonders; where morning dawns, where evening fades, you call forth songs of joy." (Psalm 65:8)

Birdhouse:

"Because you are my helper, I sing for joy in the shadow of your wings." (Psalm 63:7)

For the Birds:

"Morning" doves will eat from large bird feeders, but prefer to eat on the ground. Sprinkling a few seeds around your feeders is like putting out the welcome mat for them.

Out of the Nest

Walking in our yard one afternoon, I was bombarded by a female robin. I ducked while she dove and swooped. Looking down at my feet, I saw a baby robin scurry out of the way. Its tiny breast was a downy patch of brown spots.

Backing away, I looked up; high in the branches was the nest with two other little ones peeking over the edge. The bird in the brambles was too young to be out of the nest, but it was too high for me to help return him to safety.

At sunset, I watched the mother robin shoo her baby back into the underbrush before she returned to the nest. I prayed the Lord would protect the one hidden in the woods.

Early the next morning, the baby robin was out of hiding. The mother divided her time between the little ones above and the lonely one below. She scolded her grounded baby when he got too far away. He responded by scurrying for cover.

I watched this routine for four days. On the fifth morning, the mother sat on the ground surrounded by three hungry youngsters. She was busy teaching them to fly. I watched their flight practice, which was simple—they flew when she chased them. Eventually, all of them were perched on a branch beside her.

There's no way for me to know if the baby robin was pushed out by a sibling or decided on his own to leave the safety of the nest. Either way, the little one was in serious danger from hungry predators. Unable to fly, he needed to heed the much wiser voice of his mother—even if meant hiding in a thorny bush.

Sometimes we choose to do things that look good, or we let ourselves be convinced we can do things God has warned us against, and other times, we intentionally jump into circumstances we know we don't belong in. No matter how we get there, we're vulnerable to attack.

The Bible warns us that we too have an enemy prowling around waiting to devour us. He wants to destroy our faith, our walk, and our lives. (See 1 Peter 5:8). However, like the mother robin, the Bible also tells us that God is faithful and will protect us. When we call out to Him, we know He will hear us. One of my favorite verses, Psalm 27:5, says, "For he will conceal me there when troubles come; he will hide me in his sanctuary."

In good times and bad, there's no better place than to be under His protection.

Bird Feeder:

"But the Lord is faithful, and he will strengthen you and protect you from the evil one" (2 Thessalonians 3:3)

Birdbath:

"I am praying to you because I know you will answer, O God. Bend down and listen as I pray. Show me your unfailing love in wonderful ways. By your mighty power you rescue those who seek refuge from their enemies." (Psalm 17:5-7 NLT)

Birdhouse:

"You are my hiding place; you will protect me from trouble and surround me with songs of deliverance." (Psalm 32:7)

For the Birds:

Robins enjoy a bite of fruit now and then. They like soft fruits like apples and berries. In bitter cold, they will eat meal worms provided by compassionate humans. Robins can survive moderately cold weather, if there is a good food supply. They will also eat raisins soaked in water.

Ringo

In the '70s, when Beatlemania filled the airwaves, my family had our own personal drummer. Every day, a redheaded woodpecker we called Ringo sat on the edge of an empty oil drum. Suddenly, he would beat the rusted metal. The sound reverberated through the neighborhood. He didn't seem to mind us watching him from a close proximity, and he apparently could not hear our approach. I often worried he would get a headache or even suffer brain damage. Later, I learned God created all woodpeckers with special shock absorbers in their heads.

Sometimes life feels as futile as Ringo's banging on that empty oil drum. We work, strive, and try—all to no avail. This leaves us frustrated, weary, discouraged, and wondering where in the world God is.

We forget that He is the God who has promised never to leave or forsake us, and even more important, we can't escape His presence. Consider His words in Psalm 139:7–10, 13–14, 16–18:

"Where can I go from your Spirit? Where can I flee from your presence? If I go up to the heavens, you are there; if I make my bed in the depths, you are there. If I rise on the wings of the dawn, if I settle on the far side of the sea, even there your hand will guide me, your right hand will hold me fast."

So why do we feel so far away from Him sometimes? Could it be that in all our doing, we forget the importance of being?

When I'm weary in my soul, worn out from trying, and sick of striving, I realize it's often because I've lost sight of the reason for my doing: to please God. This means I need time to be quiet in His presence— to remember who He is, what He's done for me, and how He wants me to use my abilities, talent, and time for His glory.

For those of us who are doers by nature, we thrive on being busy, involved, and working. When we do for the right reasons and the right Person, we experience a healthy tired. When we lose sight of Him, we end up exhausted and ineffective.

At first glance, Ringo's actions seemed useless— even silly. He wasn't making any headway that we could see. I think he enjoyed beating on that rusty old oil drum. Maybe he liked the way it felt, the sound, or just making noise in the sunshine. He was being a red-headed woodpecker.

Looking back, his actions seem joyful. In the process of being what he was, the doing part came naturally. He wasn't striving, or trying, or weary. His feathers shone in the sunshine, and his body showed that the rest of the day he was finding nutrition. I know it's possible he was trying to out-do the other guys in the neighborhood for a lady woodpecker's appreciation, but whatever motivated him, it looked like he was having a great time, and it was contagious to the humans in his world.

As a doer I have lots of ideas and plans for all the things I want to do. On my own, I might do okay, but the result is a lingering fatigue and discontent. When I give what I do to God, the work I accomplish is my best, and the result is energy and success as defined by Him.

Bird Feeder:

"And whatever you do, whether in word or deed, do it all in the name of the Lord Jesus, giving thanks to God the Father through him." (Colossians 3:17)

"Whatever you do, work at it with all your heart, as working for the Lord, not for human masters, since you know that you will receive an inheritance from the Lord as a reward. It is the Lord Christ you are serving." (Colossians 3:23-24)

Birdbath:

"Commit to the LORD whatever you do, and he will establish your plans." (Proverbs 16:3)

Birdhouse:

"So whether you eat or drink or whatever you do, do it all for the glory of God." (1 Corinthians 10:31)

For the Birds:

Birds love a fresh water and bathing. Keeping the birdbath clean is essential to their health. I scrub ours once a week, using dish soap and a large brush. To keep water fresh longer, there are many natural products you can purchase where you buy your bird seed. These are usually inexpensive, but be sure they are safe not only for birds and wild animals, but also for the small children who will be fascinated by the water as well as all domestic pets.

Same Time Next Year

For three years, a pair of tree swallows returned to the nest they had built under our deck. They anchored the mud and twig bowl on a beam outside our basement window—the perfect place for watching them.

With the arrival of each spring, they diligently fixed the damage winter had done to their summer home. After a few days of busy work, they slowed down. Sitting on a deck beam or perched in a nearby tree, they watched and waited. Other birds sometimes tried to destroy their home, so they guarded the empty nest with diligence. In the evenings, they swooped through the air to catch the bugs so abundant in our woods. Their flight was both graceful and strategic.

Eventually, the female sat on the nest. I closed the blinds partway, leaving only room for a peek so my movements would not disturb them. Each year they hatched two young, which filled the mud nest to capacity in a short time. Both parents fed and watched over the babies. As nighttime approached, Mama settled in, making sure the little ones were under her wings, while Papa stood guard on the beam above.

The swallows carefully considered their building site. Safe placement of the nest ensured their survival. They secured a strong foundation with protection from the elements and predators.

We need to do the same with our spiritual lives. Our beliefs aren't only about what we believe, but they are about Who we believe in. The Bible tells us that for Christians, this foundation is Jesus Christ. When we anchor our faith on the One who is the Rock, we are eternally safe, and we are able to build a faith that cannot be washed away by anything this world sends our way.

Jesus said, "'The one who hears my words and does not put them into practice is like a man who built a house on the ground without a foundation. The moment the torrent struck that house, it collapsed and its destruction was complete.'" (Luke 6:49)

Here is the promise: if we hear and do what Jesus taught, He says we will be "like a man building a house, who dug down deep and laid the foundation on rock. When a flood came, the torrent struck that house but could not shake it, because it was well built." (Luke 6:48)

Each spring, the swallows collect new materials to rebuild their home after the wear and tear of winter storms. Sometimes all that is left is a small circle where they laid the foundation of mud, sticks, and grass. Other years, even that is taken away. But, the wise birds know that in the past, the beam or branch they chose before is where they want to anchor their nest again.

The Bible tells us, that in this world, we will have troubles, but that Jesus has overcome the world. (See John 16:33 below) This is the truth with a promise that if we choose to believe in, cling to, and grow on we will have peace in the storms.

Bird Feeder:

"As for God, his way is perfect: the LORD's word is flawless; he shields all who take refuge in him. For who is God besides the LORD? And who is the Rock except our God? It is God who arms me with strength and keeps my way secure." (Psalm 18:30-32)

Birdbath:

"I have told you these things, so that in me you may have peace. In this world you will have trouble. But take heart! I have overcome the world." (John 16:33)

Birdhouse:

"Truly he is my rock and my salvation; he is my fortress, I will never be shaken." (Psalm 62:2)

For the Birds:

Tree swallows will nest in a box house that has a base of 5" x 5" with an opening of 1". The hole should be 5" from the bottom of the nest.

Scout

A whistle and banging at the kitchen window
interrupted my quiet time. Outside, a Baltimore
oriole perched on the window ledge, looking for his
favorite treat in the spot I usually put jelly when the
orioles come. I wondered if this was the same bird
that had visited me last year. How else would he
have known where the jelly had been? I filled the
dish to the top with his favorite flavor—grape.

As I stepped outside, he flew to a nearby branch,
whistling cheerfully. We almost collided when I
turned to hurry away, and he flew straight to the
bowl now suspended on a string. For a week, he was
the only oriole in the yard, and I wondered if he was
the one who was blazing the trail for the others to
follow.

I called him Scout. I talked to him as he sat unafraid
on the other side of the screen, eating jelly and
preening his bright orange and black feathers. A few
days later, the yard was filled with the whistling call
of other orioles.

Keeping the jelly dishes full was a daily ritual. If I
didn't, Scout banged on the window with his beak to
remind me.

Waiting for Scout to return, I thought of how much
courage it takes to be a forerunner for others.
Sometimes this means to go into the dangerous
territory ahead of others for their protection.

I heard the story of a young man named Steve, who served the United States in the Vietnam War. He told of how his troop had to walk through dangerous minefields. Each soldier was to take his turn being the point man, but few had the nerve to withstand the pressure. When Steve's turn came, he prayed in the name of Jesus for God to lead them safely through the dangerous fields. The other men had so much confidence in Steve's God that they asked him to continue to lead them with his faith, to which he bravely agreed. They all returned home safely at the end of the war.

Steve wasn't the one who knew where the mines were buried, but he had a personal relationship with the One who did know where they were hidden. Steve boldly followed Jesus, and others gratefully followed him to the Prize.

Bird Feeder:

"The fear of the LORD is the beginning of wisdom; all who follow his precepts have good understanding." (Psalm 111:10)

Birdbath:

"He reached down from on high and took hold of me; he drew me out of deep waters. He rescued me from my powerful enemy, from my foes, who were too strong for me." (Psalm 18: 16-17)

Birdhouse:

"I sought You, Lord, and You answered me; You delivered me from all my fears." (Psalm 34:4)

For the Birds:

Orioles love grape jelly. Chickadees, cardinals, warblers, downy woodpeckers, and nuthatches all take their turns for a bite of this sweet delicacy.

Stolen Fish

The dolphin pool at the park was crowded with tourists. I waited in line for the fish stand to open. The sign at the window warned customers to protect their purchases from the seagulls. After buying three containers of small silver fish, I stacked them carefully in one hand and covered them with the other.

Immediately, after I stepped away from the shelter of the building, they attacked. One gull swooped at my face; when I moved my hand to protect myself, another knocked the containers to the ground. Their assault seemed choreographed. The vendor and many visitors heard my cry. The gull diving for my face had struck my hand, and it was bleeding. I washed my hands at a nearby faucet, and the fish vendor brought three more containers to me. I made it safely to the pool where our nephews and niece waited to feed the dolphins.

The dolphins seemed to know how to out-maneuver the pesky birds and got the fish every time. One even begged to have his tummy scratched, and we all obliged him.

Stepping back, I watched the gulls hovering over the fish shack. The birds lurked on the sidelines. They were bullies, raucous, and ready to take advantage of the humans who wanted to feed the dolphins and not them. Although sea gulls are intelligent and sometimes fun to watch, their aggressive, demanding behavior that day made me wish they'd go back to the ocean where they came from. Eventually, we moved on, but not before I grudgingly admitted to myself that the sly birds were effective and efficient at fishing—on land and sea.

God sometimes uses this memory to remind me that He put me here to fish too—for the souls He longs to save. Sometimes that means sharing my life and what I believe with people who live outside my comfort zone.

Jesus came to reach people who were alienated from God. He described this process to a group of rugged fishermen and invited them to join Him in becoming "fishers of men" (see Mark 1:16-18 below) These men were so drawn to Jesus that the Bible tells us they immediately left all they had and followed Him. They walked the highways and byways with Jesus to seek and save the lost.

Knowing that His time on earth would be brief, Jesus taught twelve men to share the Good News that God had made a way for us to come to Him through trusting, and believing in Jesus. They were to teach others to spread the message, and because of God's mercy, over the past two thousand plus years, this love for fishing for lost souls is still passed on to each new believer.

I came to Christ because a man named Carl Calloway loved fishing for souls the way Jesus did. Through this man's testimony of faith, Jesus caught me in His net of love, and I was saved.

If your soul hasn't found the saving love of Jesus, Acts 16:31 says, "Believe in the Lord Jesus, and you will be saved. . ."

If by faith you have believed in Jesus, rejoice!

Bird Feeder:

"Everyone who calls on the name of the Lord will be saved." (Romans 10:13)

Birdbath:

"As Jesus walked beside the Sea of Galilee, he saw Simon and his brother Andrew casting a net into the lake, for they were fishermen. 'Come, follow me,' Jesus said, 'and I will send you out to fish for people.' At once they left their nets and followed him." (Mark 1:16-18)

Birdhouse:

"Jesus answered, 'I am the way and the truth and the life. No one comes to the Father except through me.'" (John 14:6)

"Salvation is found in no one else, for there is no other name under heaven given to mankind by which we must be saved." (Acts 4:12)

For the Birds:

Seagulls and pelicans often follow inland rivers and settle on lakes during their migratory flights. For a taste of coastal birding, check your regional bird calendars to see when these seawater birds might be passing through your state. Pelicans and swans can be seen in the fall and winter months as far north as Minnesota.

The Brown Thrashers

I watched a rusty-brown thrasher, and his mate, carry twigs and grass into the messy branches of a brush pile nearby. The normally shy birds stopped occasionally to watch me with their bright yellow eyes as I cleaned my garden. A couple of days later, the male sat on a branch above the nesting spot while the female rested in the twig cup. She moved and revealed five tiny eggs.

One warm morning while planting seeds, I heard a tiny pecking sound. The thrashers watched from above the nest. I moved closer and saw a recently hatched baby thrasher. The other eggs bumped and cracked as the babies inside worked to release themselves from their protective shells. Soon the nest was filled with the demanding cries of newborns.

The next morning, the brush pile was silent. The nest was empty. I sat on the edge of my flowerbed staring at the tiny brown cup tucked in the branches. An old hurt surfaced unexpectedly. My friend Pam and her husband Chuck have five living children and two tiny ones in heaven. Jenna and Ryan were born only to live a few hours.

The missing birds caused me to finally face the death of two children whose tender smiles I would not see and giggles I would not hear. Pam and Chuck grieved deeply, yet they never quit trusting God. But how?

I looked into the clear blue sky and asked out loud, "Why, God?" He was silent. Life went on around me as the tree swallows dipped and dived to catch insects. A spider worked on a lace web between two blossoms. Hummingbirds sipped sugar water from their feeder. Butterflies and bees worked the flowers for nectar.

Determined to get an answer, I waited.

A verse I learned a long time before (See Proverbs 3:5) whispered to my heart, "Trust in the LORD with all your heart and lean not on your own understanding."

I put my head on my knees and sobbed. "But it doesn't make sense, Lord. I just don't get it," I whispered.

He answered with His words in John 14:1: "Do not let your hearts be troubled. Trust in God; trust also in me."

Jesus used this verse to comfort His disciples as He told them of heaven. He knew He would be leaving them; and in His concern for them, He promised them a gift, a Comforter—His Spirit. I felt this deep truth fill my soul as God's Holy Spirit comforted my heart. I heard the still small voice of God as He spoke to me through His Word.

Relying on the hope of heaven, the truth of God's Word, and the comfort of the Holy Spirit, Pam and Chuck survived the grief they felt. They trusted God even when their loss hurt more than any other human experience. Clinging to His promises, they continued to live for God, even when circumstances didn't make sense.

I stood up, stiff, sunburned, and sweat soaked. "Okay, Lord, I trust You." With the decision made, I walked away from the empty nest, sad, but peaceful in my soul.

Birdbath:

"In you, LORD my God, I put my trust." (Psalm 25:1)

Bird Feeder:

"Commit everything you do to the LORD. Trust him, and he will help you." (Psalm 37:5 (NLT)

Birdhouse:

"The LORD is good, a refuge in times of trouble." (Nahum 1:7)

For the Birds:

Hummingbirds are attracted to brightly colored tubular flowers. Plant a variety of flowers that will keep your garden blooming from spring to fall. Hollyhock, butterfly bush, cardinal flowers, larkspur, morning glory, petunias, phlox, trumpet vines, salvia, zinnias, and lantanas are easy to grow, heat resistant flowers that will keep birds and butterflies visiting your yard.

The Bluebirds

While weeding around the wild rose bushes, I saw a
bluebird fly into a house that my husband had put up
the previous fall. Sparrows had already inspected
this plain wood house on the metal pole in my
garden, but I really hoped the shy blue and orange
birds would live there. They did.

The birds and I worked the garden together. I was in
charge of weeds while they were my pest-control
team. I worked one section of the large flowerbed;
the birds hunted for grubs, bugs, and moths for their
young. The bees joined us in working the
coneflower, daisy, blanket flower, flax, poppy,
yarrow, wild rose, and black-eyed Susan blossoms. I
sometimes sat on the bench and the male bluebird sat
on a nearby branch. Break time!

The friendly birds didn't mind my presence, singing,
or praying out loud. For some reason, they trusted
me. Together we enjoyed our mini-prairie of
blossoms. My garden duties that summer did more
than keep the garden free of weeds. Prayer weeded
out my worries, sorrows, and chaos. Peace, comfort,
and joy were encouraged to bloom. I left each day
with an aching and sweating body, but my soul was
renewed.

Surrounded by the beauty of the flowers and the
acceptance of the gentle birds, God touched my life,
strengthened my faith, and tenderly taught me about
Himself. While the bluebirds and I worked the

garden, the flowers did what they do best—they grew. So did I.

Bird Feeder:

"Guide me in your truth and teach me, for you are God my Savior, and my hope is in you all day long." (Psalm 25:5)

Birdbath:

"The earth is filled with your love, LORD; teach me your decrees." (Psalm 119:64)

Birdhouse:

"But grow in the grace and knowledge of our Lord and Savior Jesus Christ. To him be glory both now and forever! Amen." (2 Peter 3:18)

For the Birds:

Bluebird houses are available at most garden supply stores. They need a floor area that is 4" x 4" with an entrance 8" from the bottom that is 1⅜" wide. Mount the house on a pole from 3' to 6' above the ground within 50' of a tree, fence, or other appropriate perch where the male can watch the opening of the hole when his family is nesting.

The Cold Snap

My Grandma Pater lived alone in a tiny country house with four rooms and a porch. Outside she had a big yard, and a small orchard filled with golden plum trees. The old pump on her farm had the coldest water I had ever tasted. She didn't have pets, but sometimes for company and recreation, she raised a few geese or sheep.

Staying overnight meant sleeping in her combination kitchen/living room on the hide-a-bed. Usually she woke me up by tickling me with a long pheasant feather, but one morning loud peeps brought me suddenly out of a deep sleep. The sound came from a box by the big heater. Inside were little yellow puffs of down. Because the weather had turned cold and icy in the night, Grandma had gathered the goslings from their mothers and brought them indoors. The parent birds would survive the cold snap, but she knew the little ones needed this extra protection.

Most mornings Grandma fried eggs with lacy whites and hard yolks for me. But that morning she mixed corn mash and fed the yellow peeping babies, instead. The silly geese walked in their food, splashed in the water, and bickered with each other. When the more aggressive ones had eaten, Grandma picked them up and put them in a clean box, giving the others a chance. Soon all the babies made the transition and were napping.

Then it was time for my breakfast.

The weather warmed up after a couple of days, and Grandma carried the growing geese outside. I worried the mother geese would not take their babies back, but Grandma's protection seemed to have worked for everyone when the time of crisis was over. The mothers welcomed their goslings back with honks, and soon they were all pecking at the food and mash. Their reunion was uncomplicated.

All of us experience storms in life and need a place of refuge. When we turn to Him, God cares for us as gently as my loving grandmother cared for the goslings. Oh let us run to the One who loves us more than we can imagine *before* the storm clouds of trouble gather or the winds of sorrow blow! However, if like the baby goslings, we find the storm upon us, we are not alone—He is always with us, with His wings spread wide open, offering us a safe haven of protection.

Bird Feeder:

"Let all who take refuge in you be glad; let them ever sing for joy. Spread your protection over them, that those who love your name may rejoice in you." (Psalm 5:11)

Birdbath:

"He will cover you with his feathers, and under his wings you will find refuge; his faithfulness will be your shield and rampart." (Psalm 91:4)

Birdhouse:

"I will dwell in the Your shadow—for You are my refuge and my fortress—the God I trust." (Psalm 91:1)

For the Birds:

Although most birds will eat snow, it's nice to provide them with open water in the winter. Special heaters can be purchased for the birdbath to keep water from freezing. Another option is to bury a basin of water at ground level. It will not freeze as quickly as above-ground water sources since ground temperatures stay close to 40° even when air temperatures drop to freezing.

The Cowbird

A family of cardinals came to the feeders late one afternoon. The babies had tufts of fluff mixed in with their new feathers. Three of the little birds were soft beige tinged with red, and one was brown. A mother cowbird had abandoned a single egg in the cardinal's nest when no one was looking. (This is a common cowbird practice.)

The faithful redbirds sat on the strange egg and fed the young brown bird, never questioning his right to be there. Instinct told them that his survival depended on what they could give him.

Already bigger than his adoptive parents, he demanded the lion's share of their attention. However, the wise parents kept track of each bite they gave their young and taught them all to eat. The adult birds gave each of their crew a bite, then waited for their young to feed themselves. They gently touched the younger birds' beaks affectionately, including the cowbird's. Not one of the cardinals was uncomfortable with the bigger bird, and they accepted him as their own. He was family.

Sleek feathers soon replaced the fluff. The young drop-off and his nest mates were ready to live as adult birds in the woods. One day, another bird wearing the same shades of brown showed up at the feeder and left with the two-toned brown "redbird."

Like the cowbird, we are God's adopted children through our faith in Jesus Christ. Though Jesus came as the promised Savior to the Jewish people, God accepts all those who receive Jesus as their Lord. God does not look at the color of our external details, but at the faith in our hearts.

Those who put their hope in the risen Christ are made joint-heirs to all the provisions made for God's royal family. He feeds those who believe His Word, warms us with His promises, nurtures us to maturity, and urges us to work together as the body of Christ.

Bird Feeder:

"There is neither Jew nor Gentile, neither slave nor free, nor is there male and female, for you are all one in Christ Jesus. If you belong to Christ, then you are Abraham's seed, and heirs according to the promise." (Galatians 3:28-29)

Birdbath:

"Now you are the body of Christ, and each one of you is a part of it." (1 Corinthians 12:27)

Birdhouse:

"Consequently, you are no longer foreigners and strangers, but fellow citizens with God's people and also members of his household, built on the foundation of the apostles and prophets, with Christ Jesus himself as the chief cornerstone. In him the whole building is joined together and rises to become a holy temple in the Lord. And in him you too are being built together to become a dwelling in which God lives by his Spirit." (Ephesians 2:19-22)

For the Birds:

Many birds enjoy peanut butter. A good way to serve it is to smear it onto a pinecone, then roll it in mixed birdseed. Tie a string to the top and hang the cone from a tree or pole. Unsalted peanuts in the shells are a welcome treat for blue jays, squirrels, and woodpeckers.

The Fallen Nest

After a terrible storm, I walked through our yard and picked up branches. Under a tall oak tree, I saw a tiny nest made from thin blades of grass. The fragile abode had been blown about by the strong winds but was still intact. It was lined with long, stiff horsehair from Holly across the road and with soft fur from our dog Smokey, a husky.

Inside the dog-hair lining were indentations where two little eggs had once rested. Humbled, I realized I had unknowingly provided the bird parents with some of the building supplies for their home. They had gathered mowed grass from our yard, and picked up bits of dog hair that had floated from the brush into the breeze.

After my discovery, I decided to provide more nesting materials for the birds and wild animals who live in our woods. Sometimes I get to watch them sort through scraps of yarn, dog hair, and bit of string I cut into different lengths.

Life is full of opportunities for us to contribute to the lives of others. A bag of clothes for victims of a disaster, a box of food to a homeless shelter, a word of encouragement to someone with a downcast expression can be like a drink of cold water to a parched soul. These small gifts can be pivotal in the life of someone needing strength to get through yet another difficult day.

My grandma Joy was an example of one who provided. She had very little herself, but believed that was no excuse. She visited people in the hospital and nursing homes who she knew had no one, gave food to those who had children to feed, and a friendly smile to all she met.

Jesus said blessed are those who fed Him when He was hungry, gave Him a drink when He was thirsty and hospitality when He was a stranger. He said those who clothed Him, cared for Him when He was sick, and visited Him in prison would be given their inheritance that was prepared for them since the creation of the world. When asked, "Lord, when did we see you in these conditions so that we could do these things for you?" He explained, "Whatever you did for one of the least of these brothers of mine, you did for me." (Matthew 25:40).

The little nest now sits in my hutch, reminding me of the promise in Ephesians 6:7–8 that whatever I do, if I do it with my whole heart as if I were serving the Lord, He will reward my efforts as only He can.

Bird Feeder:

"God is able to do more than all we ask or imagine, according to His power that is at work within us." (see Ephesians 3:20)

Birdbath:

"But when you give to the needy, do not let your left hand know what your right hand is doing, so that your giving may be in secret. Then your Father, who sees what is done in secret, will reward you." (Matthew 6:3–4)

Birdhouse:

"The generous will themselves be blessed, for they share their food with the poor." (Proverbs 22:9)

For the Birds:

A lovely gift for someone in a nursing home is a bird feeder mounted outside their window. This provides nutrition for the birds and hours of entertainment for your friend or family member. Please don't expect the nursing home staff to refill the feeder—you can easily do this on your next visit.

The Old Oak Tree

The temperature dipped below zero, and my dogs
needed to come in the house from their kennel. I
slipped on my boots, but not my coat, and stepped
outside. As the door slammed shut, I groaned—I was
locked out.

On our little country road, I was the only one home,
and no extra keys lay hidden under any rocks. I
climbed in my car, shivering and praying for a way
into my house. Out in the cold again, I tried to break
in without doing any damage, but nothing would
budge. I headed back for the car to escape the bitter
chill of the wind.

My teeth chattering, I prayed, asking the Lord for a
blessing. I looked around the winter wonderland and
noticed something moving on the oak tree next to the
car. A bird with a curved bill blinked at me and went
back to work on the rugged bark. A brown creeper! I
had been hoping for a long time to see this little
feathered creature. He looked at me again, then flew
away. Seeing the bird was fun, but the cold was
steadily creeping into my body. Something had to be
done.

With no other choice, I headed for the basement door
and did what the actors on TV do when they are in
this situation—I bashed the door in with my foot.
The heat inside the house washed over my cold face.

Bracing up the door, I smiled. God didn't
miraculously unlock the door, but I did see an

unexpected blessing on the bark of the oak. Gratitude for His kindness flooded my soul. I put on the teapot and thanked the Lord for our furnace.

Snuggling on the couch with my dogs, thanking God for strong legs and a weak door jam, I remembered when I was fifteen and wanted to know Him as a person—not just about Him. I paced my bedroom and asked the God of the universe to send someone who knew Him to me. Like a lot of teens, I was silently afraid of the multitude of changes growing up held for me.

Although I wasn't sure God had time for the prayers of a teenage girl, I asked anyway.

A couple of days later, I opened our front door and met Pastor Carl Calloway. In the next few weeks, I learned about Jesus and of God's great love for me. God not only heard my prayer; He answered it.

On that cold day when God sent me a brown creeper to bless me, I celebrated my salvation again, thanksgiving spilling from my heart into a prayer of praise.

Then, I limped to the phone to tell Jon about the damaged door, the bird, and how God used those things to tell me again how much He loved me. I watched him fix the door with a smile on his face. The project was an inconvenience, but Jon didn't seem to mind.

Bird Feeder:

"And without faith it is impossible to please God, because anyone who comes to him must believe that he exists and that he rewards those who earnestly seek him." (Hebrews 11:6)

Birdbath:

"Those who know your name trust in you, for you, LORD, have never forsaken those who seek you." (Psalm 9:10)

Birdhouse:

"Glory in his holy name; let the hearts of those who seek the LORD rejoice. Look to the LORD and his strength; seek his face always." (Psalm 105:3-4)

For the Birds:

Many birds enjoy fruit especially oranges and apples. It's easy to cut these fruits into sections or slices and put them where the birds will quickly find them. There are special feeders for these tasty treats that will keep the fruit clean and allow the birds to perch while they eat.

The Swan

One warm Sunday afternoon, my parents took my little brother and me to the lake. Clutched in our hands were bright polka-dot bread bags. We were going to feed the geese. I loved being surrounded by the big birds and had often watched them eat right out of my dad's hand. That day I was going to try it, too.

To my delight, the swans came to us, and to my five-year-old body, they were huge. In the water, they were graceful and seemed lighter than air. But on land they waddled clumsily on black legs that seemed too skinny to hold up their big, white bodies. Dad offered the first bite of bread to a swan that gobbled it down.

I eagerly reached in the bag and grabbed a piece of bread. Tearing off a corner, I held it out for the swan, but I forgot to let go of it. The swan's mouth closed around my fingers and pulled. A short tug-of-war began. I wanted my finger back, but in my fear forgot to release the treat I'd offered the bird.

The swan eventually got the bread. I got hissed at and a sore finger. The skin wasn't broken, but my heart was shocked. Tears filled my eyes as my concerned parents checked me over. "But why did the swan bite me?" I asked, tears running down my cheeks.

My heart was hurting at what I perceived was the rejection of the beautiful creature in front of me.

While the white bird waited for another bite of bread, Dad explained that in order for the swan and me to have a good relationship, I needed to let go of the bread. Then he showed me that I had two options: I could put pieces of bread on the ground, or if I offered the bread in my open palm, the swan could take the bread without hurting me.

Wanting to be friends with all things wild, I chose to offer the treats with my hand wide open. My tears evaporated, and the bread bag was soon empty.

Remembering that encounter, I realize many of us try to manage our lives with our inner fists clenched. We suffer from tense jaws, sore shoulders, pain in our necks, and headaches. We live in a constant state of stress and forget that release is only a prayer away. And sometimes when we do remember to pray, we utter the words unwilling to let go leaving our prayer time more tense than before.

It's like the swan and me; when we offer God our cares, He's willing to take them, but in order for that to work, we have to release everything to Him. When we take Him our troubles resting on the open palms of our hearts, He not only hears the prayer, He is able to do something with them.

Living open-hearted doesn't guarantee us stress-free living, but we will be stronger in our faith, more settled in our minds, and healthier in our bodies.

Bird Feeder:

"Search me, God, and know my heart; test me and know my anxious thoughts. See if there is any offensive way in me, and lead me in the way everlasting." (Psalm 139:3-4)

Birdbath:

"Trust in the LORD with all your heart and lean not on your own understanding." (Proverbs 3:5)

Birdhouse:

"Love the Lord your God with all your heart and with all your soul and with all your mind and with all your strength." (Mark 12:30)

For the Birds:

Keep a journal listing the birds you have seen. Record where you were, what they were doing, and what you were thinking at the time. Or simply mark your sightings on a calendar as you noticed birds you haven't seen before, or when familiar ones return. Record significant birding dates such as how often you buy seed, put up new houses, and see babies at the feeders. It's fun to read your calendar notes or journal on New Year's Eve.

The Thank-You Song

As dusk settled over the woods, the urgent call of a cardinal broke the silence. A male redbird fluttered at the kitchen window where I was drying the dishes. My husband and I went outside to see what was disturbing him.

He flew just ahead of us, continuing his agitated cry. He landed near a female on a nest. It took a moment for our eyes to adjust to the twilight. As we scanned the trees, we found the source of the bird's emergency. Almost invisible in the tree above the nest sat a huge owl.

We watched for awhile; then the owl blinked his yellow eyes, opened his wings, and glided silently away. We turned to go back in the house, amazed that the cardinal had led us to his home.

The redbird followed us to the house, where we stopped by the door. He sat in the brambles near us and sang to us again. This time the melody was lovely. Jon said, "It's as if he was saying thank you." When the bird finished his solo, we watched him rejoin his family in the nest.

I returned to the dishes certain that somehow the cardinal knew we would help him. I marveled at the wonderful and mysterious ways of God.

Like the cardinal, we sometimes need help that is greater than ourselves. When we utter a desperate, often silent prayer, God is quick to respond.

Although it's hard to comprehend His abilities, He can handle the whole universe and not be too busy for you and I. Instead, He attends to the cry of our hearts.

Bird Feeder:

"I will take refuge in the shadow of your wings until the disaster has passed." (Psalm 57:1)

Birdbath:

"We wait in hope for the LORD; he is our help and our shield. In him our hearts rejoice, for we trust in his holy name." (Psalm 33:20-21)

Birdhouse:

"Because you are my help, I sing in the shadow of your wings." (Psalm 63:7)

For the Birds:

If you own a cat that frequently stalks your feeders, you may want to consider putting a bell on the cat's collar. If the stalker is a neighbor's cat, you could mention you enjoy their pet's visits, and that you' d appreciate it if they'd place a collar with a bell on their cat for your birds' sake. The bonus is you and your neighbor will know where your feline friend is too.

The Wedding Guest

Guests gathered in the woodland clearing and waited. Sunlight bathed the altar, and birds sang sweetly in the branches. Wedding music started, and we turned to watch for the bride.

From the back row, I watched in wonder as she walked the grassy aisle. Unbeknownst to her, an unexpected guest hovered behind her. Drawn by the color and fresh scent of the flowers in her hair, a male ruby-throated hummingbird joined the wedding party to escort the bride to her groom.

His emerald and ruby feathers looked like an elegant tuxedo perfect for the occasion. Her groom smiled at her, as the iridescent guest hovered nearby with mutual attentiveness to her movements. We could see the groom's joy in his eyes, as he watched her slow, graceful approach.

The moment was a sweet illustration of the mysterious relationship God offers us when we accept Jesus as Lord of our life. The Word of God likens our relationship with Christ to marriage. When we become One with the Father through faith in the Son, His Spirit indwells us. The Spirit is the Advocate (helper, teacher, intercessor, and comforter) Jesus promises in John 14 (see below). Like the hummingbird at the wedding, the Holy Spirit draws our attention to God and giving the world a glimpse of His radiant love through us.

One day Jesus will stand before the world with those who love Him and say, "Behold, I present my bride, my church, whom I love more than my own flesh. I nourished her, carefully protected her and cherished her, and now look at her glorious splendor." (see Ephesians 5:27) All those at the wedding ceremony will live with Him forever as eternal members of His household.

Bird Feeder:

"Let us rejoice and be glad and give him glory! For the wedding of the Lamb has come, and his bride has made herself ready." (Revelation 19:7)

Birdbath:

"But the Advocate, the Holy Spirit, whom the Father will send in my name, will teach you all things and will remind you of everything I have said to you." (John 14: 26)

Birdhouse:

"Surely goodness and love will follow me all the days of my life, and I will dwell in the house of the LORD forever." (Psalm 23:6)

For the Birds:

Some birds, like scarlet tanagers and yellow warblers are drawn to running water. Purchasing an inexpensive fountain, or setting your hose up to dribble into your current birdbath is like putting out the welcome mat for these lovely songsters. It takes a few days for them to feel comfortable coming this close to humans, but it is worth the effort. If you plant flowers around your birdbath, they will get watered as well. Letting the water run in the early morning and evening are usually enough. The other birds who frequent your feeders also enjoy the sound and movement of running water. If you sit nearby, the sound is soothing to the human soul as well.

Turkey Buzzards

One summer a family of turkey buzzards roosted single file on the peak of our roof. I was used to watching these large birds from afar. They gracefully circled the skies overhead in search of food. Our company would often mistake them for eagles, but a close view of them reveals that nothing could be further from the truth. Their red, featherless heads, slumped shoulders, and greasy, ratty feathers aren't beautiful. A friend of mine declared when he saw them, "They are *ugly* birds!"

However, God created turkey buzzards with an essential job, and their appearance is part of His plan. While their circling just appears to be lazy circles, they are systematic hunters. Although their beaks and talons are not designed to attack live flesh, they eat animals killed along the roads and those that die from natural causes. Internally, they have been given the unique ability to kill any virus or bacteria they digest, and yet their own droppings are disease free. As cleanup crews, they fight the spread of infectious disease in our woods and on country roads that might otherwise hurt humans.

They are dependable parents who stay with their young to teach them the ways of survival. These communal birds live roost together, often in the same tree, perched on the same branch for most of their lives. They can venture two hundred miles in search of food, then return to their designated limb two weeks later. They are also generous birds; when a large meal is found, such as the carcass of a dead cow or deer, they somehow communicate to other roosts of vultures that live as far as thirty miles away to share their find and help with the cleanup. They are gentle to each other and those around them.

Turkey buzzards are friendly to people, too, often choosing to live as close to humans as possible. Many have been known to befriend joggers and children walking to bus stops by showing up each day at their scheduled venue. Wounded birds in rehabilitation grow so attached to their caretaker, they follow them around like pet dogs. How sad for us if we choose to judge these intelligent and loving birds by their looks.

Turkey buzzards thrive as they show themselves friendly, serve their community, and do it all faithfully. While society often ignores or disregards the unattractive, these gangly birds remind us that beauty is a way of life and not just our physical attributes. Sometimes we have to look a little deeper to find the treasure hidden within all of God's creation. Although we often miss it in the social clamor, there is peace when we endeavor to live gently, looking for the beauty in others.

Bird Feeder:

"Be completely humble and gentle; be patient, bearing with one another in love." (Ephesians 4:2)

Birdbath:

"The Lord does not look at the things people look at. People look at the outward appearance, but the Lord looks at the heart." (1 Samuel 16:7)

Birdhouse:

"Let your gentleness be evident to all. The Lord is near." (Philippians 4:5)

For the Birds:

Sparrows are often disregarded by beginning birders. However, this family of birds displays a wonderful variety of markings. Study the field guides, and then watch closely for the subtle differences in these friendly birds. Millet or thistle on the ground will attract the song sparrow, the house sparrow, Harris's sparrow, the white-crowned, the golden crowned, and the white-throated sparrow. There are many more to be enjoyed and added to your life-list journal of birds.

Under His Wings

Several years ago, Jon took me to the island of Kauai. We rode a helicopter over the Waimea Canyon, enjoyed the beauty as rainbows danced from plunging waterfalls, and watched sea turtles, dolphins, and humpback whales play in the ocean.

And, we watched chickens. We might call them wild-range chickens, but on Kauai, they are protected. Many stories are linked to the brightly-colored fowl. The one we heard most often was that there was a large problem on the island with owners and others betting on rooster fights. After a hurricane set most of them free, the governor saw an opportunity to end the brutal practice and proclaimed them a protected species. Some swear this is true, and others insist is it a legend created to entertain gullible visitors.

Whatever the truth is, these beautiful birds roam the island freely. Although tourists are encouraged not to feed them, the birds know how to charm humans. For one little rooster, this was almost his undoing.

We were visiting one of the local sites, and were surrounded by hens, roosters, and their young. There were so many little ones, it looked like a baby chicken playground. A sudden storm blew in off the ocean and mother birds started clucking calls to their fluffy babies. Little birds who had been chasing each other, rushed to safety. Mothers stretched their wings over their little ones.

A little girl had fallen in love with one little rooster, and he was fond of her cookie crumbs. She was trying to talk her mother into letting her take him home on the airplane and strategically placing pieces of her treat behind her. He was distracted from hearing his mother's urgent calls by his desire for food.

His siblings had already gathered under the protection of their mother's wings. Their little eyes and beaks were all we could see from the safety of her water-repellent feathers. The thunder rolled, and his mother called to him again, but he continued to follow the girl. At the car, the girl's mother shooed the little bird back, and shut the door just as the storm cloud started to sprinkle us with big, warm drops. The chick's soft baby fluff was no protection from the rain, and without his mother's feathers, he could get sick and die.

No longer enticed by cookie crumbs, the little bird felt the rain, and heard his mother's now frantic cluck. He ran to her, and wiggled his way between two of his sisters directly under her breast. He turned around, and like the others, peeked out as the storm released a soaking rain.

Sometimes, I'm like this little rooster rebel. My heavenly Father knows a storm is coming, and calls out to protect me. Instead of listening to Him and turning back, I let myself get distracted. He is gracious and continues to offer His invitation to find safety in the shelter of His wings. When I finally become aware of the danger and hear His voice, I run to the protection only God provides. Although there are others there, He always has room for me.

Birdfeeder:

". . . whoever listens to me will live in safety and be at ease, without fear of harm." (Proverbs 1:33)

Birdbath:

"He will cover you with his feathers, and under his wings you will find refuge; his faithfulness will be your shield and rampart." (Psalm 91:4 NIV)

Birdhouse:

"The name of the LORD is a fortified tower; the righteous run to it and are safe." (Proverbs 18:10)

For the Birds:

Downy woodpeckers, chickadees, and flickers will often drink nectar from hummingbird and oriole feeders. Don't worry about them taking too much sugar water from their much smaller neighbors, the hummers will chase them away when it's their turn.

Woody

I thought Woody the Woodpecker was an
exaggerated, make-believe character, so I was
surprised the first time I saw the large, red-crested
bird on our oak tree. The bird was obviously a
woodpecker, but he was the size of a crow or bigger.
His powerful moves against the tree sounded like
hammering, and wood chips flew in all directions.
He paused, cocked his head, and moved up the tree,
where he attacked a new spot.

I reached for my bird book. There he was—a
pileated woodpecker. I continued to watch him. The
bird reminded me of the pterodactyls in *The
Flintstones;* he was clumsy and prehistoric-looking.
The bugs he heard under the bark didn't stand a
chance against him. He worked the tree almost
leisurely, moving only when he exterminated the
insects in the hole he had made.

I heard a loud vibrato call in the woods; he raised his
head, answered, and flew away.

In studying more about the bird, I learned
woodpeckers help trees survive the invasion of
destructive insects. They pound out bugs in the tree
bark that would otherwise rob the trees of life-giving
sap. Within a few days, the wounds left on the tree
from the woodpecker's search for food are covered
with a healing, white substance produced by most
trees, protecting them from further damage.

We sometimes feel like the oak tree bugged by invading forces. Now and then, our lives resemble the oak tree full of invaders. In spite of our faith, we let our failures, the insults of others, disappointments, and painful memories burrow deep into our hearts. Over time, they take root leaving us feeling like there is no escape. This lie keeps us from the freedom God intends for those He loves.

As believers, we sometimes forget that like the trees pounded on by the big woodpeckers, God will heal the wounds sin, pain, sorrow, regret, or hurt have left behind.

Bird Feeder:

"We wait in hope for the LORD; he is our help and our shield. In him our hearts rejoice, for we trust in his holy name." (Psalm 33:20-21)

Birdbath:

"Let us then approach God's throne of grace with confidence, so that we may receive mercy and find grace to help us in our time of need." (Hebrews 4:16)

Birdhouse:

"Search me, God, and know my heart; test me and know my anxious thoughts. See if there is any offensive way in me, and lead me in the way everlasting." (Psalm 138: 23-24)

For the Birds:

If you have a dead tree nearby that is not where it could cause damage if it fell, keep it. Woodpeckers, flickers, nuthatches, brown creepers, and chickadees will work the tree and entertain the birdwatchers at your house.

Additional Reading:

Books (with Amazon Links)

National Geographic Backyard Guide to the Birds of North America

http://www.amazon.com/National-Geographic-Backyard-America-Guides/dp/1426207204/

Stokes Beginner's Guide to Birds: Eastern Region

http://www.amazon.com/Stokes-Beginners-Guide-Birds-Eastern/dp/0316818119/

The Stokes Field Guide to the Birds of North America

http://www.amazon.com/Stokes-Field-Guide-America-Guides/dp/0316010502/

The New Stokes Field Guide to Birds: Western Region [Paperback] Donald Stokes (Author), Lillian Stokes (Author)

http://www.amazon.com/New-Stokes-Field-Guide-Birds/dp/0316213926/

The New Stokes Field Guide to Birds: Eastern Region [Paperback]

Donald Stokes (Author), Lillian Stokes (Author)

http://www.amazon.com/New-Stokes-Field-Guide-Birds/dp/0316213934/

National Wildlife Federation Field Guide to Birds of North America

http://www.amazon.com/National-Wildlife-Federation-Field-America/dp/1402738749/

National Geographic Complete Birds of North America

http://www.amazon.com/National-Geographic-Complete-Birds-America/dp/0792241754/

About Birds: A Guide for Children Cathryn Sill (Author), John Sill (Illustrator)

http://www.amazon.com/About-Birds-A-Guide-Children/dp/1561451479/

The Audubon Backyard Birdwatcher: Birdfeeders and Bird Gardens by Robert Burton and Stephen Kress

http://www.amazon.com/Audubon-Backyard-Birdwatcher-Birdfeeders-Gardens/dp/1607104040/

A Guide to the Nests, Eggs, and Nestlings of North American Birds (Princeton Field Guides) [Paperback] Paul J. Baicich

http://www.amazon.com/Guide-Nestlings-American-Princeton-Guides/dp/0691122954/

Birds, Nests & Eggs (Take Along Guides) [Paperback] Mel Boring http://www.amazon.com/Birds-Nests-Eggs-Along-Guides/dp/155971624X/**Online Magazines:**

Birds & Blooms:

http://birdsandblooms.com/

Birdwatching: http://www.birdwatchingdaily.com/

The Audubon Society: http://birds.audubon.org/

http://www.birdwatching.com

http://www.stokesbirdsathome.com

About the Author

Joy DeKok lives on 35 acres of woods and field just outside of Pine Island, MN with her

husband Jon and their dogs, Sophie and Tucker. Joy enjoys watching and feeding the

birds as well as the other wildlife that visit the feeders and the pond in their valley. She often

blogs about what God teaches her through His creation.

To read about some of her recent adventures, visit http://www.joydekok.com and http://www.booksbyjoy.com

Joy is also the author of a novel, *Rain Dance*, a non-fiction series; *Your Life a Legacy, Your Life a Legacy For Kids, Your Life a Legacy for Teens, Poetry—Touch the World With Your Art & Soul*, and three children's books; *It Is Good, Room For Bandit*, and *Raccoon Tales.*

She's also a professional speaker and can be contacted at http://www.joydekok.com.

When she's not working, Joy enjoys time with her family and friends or traveling with Jon.

The DeKok's attend Autumn Ridge Church in Rochester, MN.

Contact Joy at: Joydekok57@gmail.com or write to her at:

10227 95th Ave NW

Pine Island, MN 55963

Also Published by Infusion Publishing

61934259R00104

Made in the USA
Columbia, SC
30 June 2019